Cowley Publications is a ministry of the brothers of the Society of Saint John the Evangelist, a monastic order in the Episcopal Church. Our mission is to provide books and resources for those seeking spiritual and theological formation. Cowley Publications is committed to developing a new generation of writers and teachers who will encourage people to think and pray in new ways about spirituality, reconciliation, and the future.

D0282321

Where You Go, I Shall

Gleanings from the Stories of Biblical Widows

Jane J. Parkerton
K. Jeanne Person
Anne Winchell Silver

Cowley Publications
Cambridge, Massachusetts

Library of Congress Cataloging-in-Publication Data:
Parkerton, Jane J., 1946–
  Where you go, I shall : gleanings from the stories of biblical widows / Jane
J. Parkerton, K. Jeanne Person, Anne Winchell Silver.
      p. cm.
  Includes bibliographical references (p.   ).
  ISBN 1-56101-237-8 (pbk. : alk. paper)
  1. Widows in the Bible. 2. Bible. O.T.—Criticism, interpretation, etc.
  I. Person, K. Jeanne, 1962– II. Silver, Anne Winchell, 1948– III. Title.
  BS1199.W7P37 2005
  220.9'2'08654—dc22

                                2005012080

Cover design: Brad Norr Design
Cover art: *Ruth and Naomi* (mural)
West London Synagogue,
London, U.K.
Bridgeman Art Library

This book was printed in the United States of America on acid-free paper.

Cowley Publications
4 Brattle Street
Cambridge, Massachusetts 02138
800-225-1534 • www.cowley.org

To Prosper, Kamal, and David

I heard a voice from heaven saying unto me, Write,
From henceforth blessed are the dead who die in the Lord:
even so saith the Spirit; for they rest from their labours.
(Revelation 14:13)

The Order for the Burial of the Dead
of the 1928 Book of Common Prayer

contents

preface

❈

THE NOVELIST TRACY CHEVALIER once confessed that she always reads book acknowledgments "looking for clues that will shed light on writers and their working methods and lives, as well as their connections with the real world." In this preface to our book, we suppose you, the reader, will also discover something about our faith and our relationships with God.

The idea for *Where You Go, I Shall* first came to Jeanne after a few months of gatherings of the Ruth & Naomi Circle, a support group for widows at Grace Church Brooklyn Heights. Seeing the women care for one another with great tenderness, and listening to their experiences, inspired Jeanne to imagine that a book linking biblical and contemporary experiences of widowhood might be helpful to a wider community. For their love and insights, therefore, we wish especially to thank the sister-widows of the Ruth & Naomi Circle: Dorothy, Eleanor, Joanne, Kitty, and Lesley.

Because Jeanne is not a widow, however, she knew that for the book to have an authentic voice she would need to invite someone else to write with her. Soon, she realized that the book could be even more powerful if two widows with very different experiences would agree to be co-authors. So our trinity of writers came into being.

Separately and together, we gradually cried and laughed our book into completion. Usually working quietly alone, sometimes e-mailing a selection to the others for comments, we would write our individual sections. Then, once or twice a month, the three of us gathered at one of our dining room tables, surrounded by food, pitchers of iced tea, yellow writing pads, variegated pencils, a lighted candle, and a wooden icon depicting the biblical widows Ruth and Naomi. We would go over our latest chapter sentence by sentence, page by page, negotiating revisions until all three agreed. Many times we were quite surprised by how well our individual section drafts fit together, not by our plan or intention, and we interpreted this as a grace of the Holy Spirit.

Our writing offered us an extraordinary experience of the presence of God when two or three are gathered in Christ's name. What astounded us in the writing process was the sense of God's presence not just *with*, but also *within* us. We called ourselves a trinity of writers and, truly, the Trinity seemed manifest. Jeanne was the "Creator" who originated, shaped, and set in motion the idea for the book. Anne, who is very down-to-earth and knows the practical aspects of being an author, was the "Incarnate" one. Jane's inspiring stories and poetic language stirred in our souls an awareness of the "Spirit." Our approaches complemented each other to such an extent that writing together was a pleasure.

We are grateful to Michael Wilt of Cowley Publications for his patient and wise editorial support and guidance. We also would like to thank our "test readers" who commented extensively on early drafts of this book: Judith Brilliant, who also helped us with Hebrew transliteration; Judith Dunlap; Jane Sullivan; Gladys Van Brederode; Mary Waugh; and Marjorie and William Winchell.

We would also like to express our gratitude to the community of Grace Church Brooklyn Heights for nourishing us during the various stages of our lives, for bringing us together, and for providing us with a place to explore and practice our spiritual gifts.

Because we are three in one, we also wish to thank a few people individually:

Jane

Jordan and Whitney, my daughters, who gave me reason aplenty to rise up and greet each new day, and Benjamin Gross, my son-in-law, advocate, and friend.

Bea McAfee Jordan, my mother, who gave me poetry, and Willie Albert Jordan, my father, who taught me to dream.

Kristin Conner and Will Jordan, my sister and brother, together we give voice to the memories.

Bruce, Flory, Joy, Lucy, Diane and Dick, Ronnie, Jo Ann, Nancy C., Nancy K., Priscilla, Goldy and Mary, and David, under whose wings my daughters and I found shelter.

Jeanne

Kamal Abdullah, my husband and dearest companion, who reveals God to me every moment and for whom my love is deep, passionate, and abiding.

Sandra Person Burns, Daniel Joseph Person, Mary Butler Person, and Warren Trimble Burns, my lovely parents and their spouses.

Joanna Ashworth, Gary Hellman, and Barbara Cawthorne Crafton, whose spiritual care for me during a time of transition helped to open my heart to new possibilities.

Nils Blatz, Bruce Griffith, Andrew St. John, and Michael Phillips, colleagues and teachers in the ordained ministry.

Anne

Deborah and Robert Santoro; Helayne Silver and Carl Jeser; Judith and William Dunlap; Daniel Silver; and Joshua and Justine Silver; who were so faithfully present when their father and I needed them most.

prologue

❧

Gleanings

FOR FARMERS IN THE BIBLE, to glean meant to gather, after the harvest, the very last stalks of wheat or barley still in the field, the remaining grapes in the vineyard, the few olives or figs yet on the tree. Farmers did not, however, themselves glean. Jewish law required farmers to leave a small portion of their crops unharvested for the sake of the poor:

> When you reap the harvest of your land, you shall not reap to the very edges of your field, or gather the gleanings of your harvest. You shall not strip your vineyard bare, or gather the fallen grapes of your vineyard; you shall leave them for the poor and the alien: I am the Lord your God.
> *Leviticus 19:9–10*

So it was the poor, the hungry, the outcast who would glean the fields, vineyards, and groves for what little food they could find.

Among the poor for whom the farmers thus provided were widows. In the patriarchal world of the Bible, women usually could not inherit the wealth of their fathers or husbands. If a woman bore no son and her husband died, she could fall into abject poverty. Among the last and the least in their society, widows were often in the fields at harvest time, to gather in the last and the least of the produce. One such widow,

beloved in the biblical narrative, was Ruth, who in desperation after the deaths of her husband, brother-in-law, and
father-in-law, gleaned the fields of Boaz.

Of the three women who wrote this book, only Jane grew
up on a farm, and we all have called Brooklyn, a borough of
New York City, home for many years. Our rhythms, and the
sights, smells, sounds, and tastes of our lives, are urban, not
rural. So, for us, gleaning has a powerful and personal dimension beyond its agricultural roots.

To glean can also mean to gather anything at all, little by
little, gradually. One can glean bits of information, clues for
solving a mystery, pearls of wisdom, a circle of friends.
Through a lifetime of prayer, one can glean glimpses into the
glory and beauty of God. To glean, then, is a spiritual art.
Its practice both requires and strengthens attentiveness,
patience, faithfulness, an ability to gather in what God is
offering, and an openness to the gift that comes unexpectedly.

Where You Go, I Shall is the yield of our gleanings from the
stories of widows in the Bible. Our interest grew from the
seeds of our own experience. Anne and Jane are widows, and
Jeanne is an Episcopal priest. When Anne's husband died
after a long illness, Jeanne invited several widows of our
parish, Grace Church Brooklyn Heights, to form a Ruth and
Naomi Circle, named after two widows in the Bible who care
for each other. Every month in the parish's Nativity Chapel,
where we could sit in a circle within a quiet, sacred space, we
came together for Bible study, prayer, and conversation about
the sorrows and struggles of widowhood. The stained-glass
window of the chapel features a resplendent and royal Mary
holding the baby Jesus, while Joseph, an older man, fatigued,
falls asleep with his head in his hand. The window hints,
then, of Mary's own future widowhood and the grief that will
pierce her heart. Joseph will die, and then, all too soon, Jesus.
In our Circles, as we called our gatherings, Mary was, therefore, a sister among us.

In time we discovered that many remarkable women in the
Bible are widows. Not just Mary, Ruth, and Naomi, but also
Abigail, Anna, Tamar, and Judith, and widows whose names
will never be known; all shape the course of the biblical

narrative. Touching on many different aspects of widowhood, their stories resonated with our own.

Our monthly conversations also began to offer healing. By befriending one another, we broke through the isolation of widowhood. As much as for the widows of the Bible, social alienation besets widows today. Afraid of the too-close reality of death, people, even close friends, often subtly shun widows just when we most need companionship. People seem uncomfortable hearing about our grief, about how our husbands or partners died, about how difficult it is for us to be single again, or even about the funny, joyful stories of our past loves. In our Circles we began to find the friendship our souls yearned for, as we wept and laughed, complained, hoped, brought in photographs and keepsakes, remembered.

☉ↄꙩ

This book tells the stories of widows in the Bible as well as our own stories. Each chapter begins with a meditation written by Jeanne on the story of a biblical widow. Then, Anne and Jane, individually, reflect on aspects of their own widowhood that relate to the biblical story. Their personal experiences are quite different and, so we hope, helpful.

Anne is a recent widow who knew her husband was dying. David died on April 24, 2003, after a courageous battle with cancer. They had been married for almost twenty-four years. David had children and grandchildren from previous marriages; Anne and David had no children together. Theirs had been an interfaith marriage; David was raised in an Orthodox Jewish home and, although no longer observant as an adult, still identified himself as Jewish.

Jane has been a widow for many years, after the sudden and unexpected death of her husband. On May 10, 1988, Prosper died of cardiac arrest while jogging that evening on the Brooklyn Bridge, leaving Jane to raise two young daughters. At the time of his death, Jane and Prosper were both members of Grace Church.

We have structured the book in this way to help you, the reader, to glean. You may wish to gather in what God has to offer through us little by little, gradually. If you are a recent widow, or someone who cares for one, you might wish first to read Anne's remembrances. If your husband or partner died many years ago, or you wish to reach out to such a widow, you might walk with Jane.

The biblical and modern stories in this book begin with the experience of death (Abigail) and the difficult emotions of the early days and weeks of widowhood (Naomi). We then explore the challenges of being a widow with, or without, children (Widow of Zarephath) and dealing with new financial circumstances (The Widow with Two Coins). Widowhood often demands great resourcefulness and may involve feelings of shame (Tamar); it may also affect our faith and our feelings about God and religion in unexpected ways (Anna). Finally, we discuss the process of emerging from intense mourning, including the rediscovery of one's power, wisdom, and sexuality (Judith), aided by the healing support of community (Ruth).

Each of Jeanne's meditations ends with prayer ideas, some specifically for widows and some for everyone. Among the ideas, some may resonate strongly for you, others not at all. We invite you to choose among them and to pray slowly, across a span of time, rather than all at once.

In gleaning, may you who are widows find yourselves becoming members of a wider circle of sister-widows who understand, support, and love one another. And whoever you are, may you discover, as we have, the astounding richness of the Bible in revealing both the concerns and the life-giving friendship of widows.

chapter one

❊

Abigail

1 Samuel 25:2–42

AMONG THE STORIES OF WIDOWS in the Bible, Abigail's brings us closest to the moment of death. Seldom do we meet a biblical widow before her husband dies. With Abigail, we not only come to know her before Nabal dies but also are privileged to accompany her as she tries courageously to prevent his death.

Abigail appears within the saga of David's rise to power. David, a successful warrior, has become famous and beloved among the people. As a mere youth, "ruddy and handsome" (1 Samuel 17:42), he had defeated the Philistine Goliath with his sling, and thereafter, as commander of King Saul's army, he won many battles against the neighboring enemy. Because of David's popularity, however, King Saul has become envious. Now the king is seeking to kill him, and David is on the run. A few hundred disreputable men have joined him: "everyone who was in distress, and everyone who was in debt, and everyone who was discontented" (22:2); they have been roaming around the countryside, hiding from King Saul, slaying Philistines for bounty, trying to survive. Presently they are camping in the wilderness of Maon near Carmel, where Abigail's husband Nabal shepherds his flock.

We are told it is the season for sheepshearing, and as with the grain harvests and grape vintages, it is a time for joyous celebration, festivity, and hospitality. Sheepshearing offers an occasion for a feast, and David and his roving band of fighters are hungry. So David sends messengers to Nabal, a wealthy man with three thousand sheep and a thousand goats, asking politely, with words of peace and friendship, for an invitation. David reminds Nabal that David's men had protected Nabal's shepherds in the field. But Nabal, a man who is "surly and mean" (1 Samuel 25:3) and whose name means "fool," insults David. "Who is David? Who is the son of Jesse? Shall I take my bread and my water and the meat that I have butchered for my shearers, and give it to men who come from I do not know where?" (25:10–11). Greatly offended, David and his men strap on their swords to avenge the insult, as a young messenger runs to the "clever and beautiful" Abigail (25:3) to warn her.

Nabal will surely die, and when he does, Abigail will be left a widow in a patriarchal society in which widows without sons are among the most poor. She will not inherit Nabal's wealth, his sheep, his goats, his land, his servants. In the very moment of his death, she will fall from being the wife of a prosperous and powerful, if unpleasant, man to being a widow who likely will have to beg for food and protection. She will lose everything. So she attempts, with all her resilience, to save her husband from death.

Without a word to her husband, and with extraordinary courage, she hurriedly puts together a gift of bread, wine, ready-dressed sheep, grain, raisins, and figs—ample food for David's men. She then steals out to David in the wilderness, sending her own young male servants ahead of her, wisely under the cover of a mountain, for if David and his men see them from afar, they might rush to kill them. When she finally reaches David's camp, she quickly falls prostrate on the ground before him to beg his mercy.

In one of the most eloquent speeches by a woman in the Bible, Abigail appeals not only to David's need to feed his hungry men but also to his theology, military reputation, literary appreciation, and faith in God's promises for him.

She begins by urging him not to become guilty of shedding blood without cause. With politic rhetoric she proclaims that God has indeed already held back David from bloodguilt: "Now then, my lord, as the LORD lives, and as you yourself live, since the LORD has restrained you from bloodguilt and from taking vengeance with your own hand, now let your enemies and those who seek to do evil to my lord be like Nabal" (1 Samuel 25:26). Her words are evocative for David, because he had only recently kept himself from similar bloodguilt in a confrontation with King Saul in the wilderness of En-gedi. The king had brought out three thousand men to seek David's life. David had hidden in a cave, and when the king, by chance, had come in privately to relieve himself, David, instead of killing the king, had stealthily cut off a corner of the king's coat. David had then gone out to King Saul and bowed before him with his face to the ground, just as Abigail is now doing. David had showed the king the piece of cloth as proof of his righteousness, proclaiming that he would not bear the guilt of shedding the king's blood: "May the LORD avenge me on you; but my hand shall not be against you. . . . May the LORD therefore be judge, and give sentence between me and you. May he see to it, and plead my cause, and vindicate me against you" (24:12,15). Whereupon the king had called David his son and openly wept. Perhaps word of this encounter between David and King Saul had spread throughout Israel, and Abigail knows of David's pangs of conscience. Regardless, she is confident of her argument's theological persuasiveness for David.

Abigail also wisely seeks to assuage David's enraged feelings over Nabal's churlish insult, "Who is David?" David was once the most celebrated figure in all Israel. People throughout the land had adored him for his military victories, sang praises to him, had great expectations for him. When as a youth David had killed the Philistine Goliath, women had come out from all the towns of Israel with tambourines and other musical instruments, singing and dancing joyfully (1 Samuel 18:6–7). Abigail was likely among them. So Nabal's question is a stinging discourtesy, suggesting that David, no longer beloved of the king, is now merely like the men who are wandering with him in the wilderness, lost men, infamous, distressed, poor, malcontent. Abigail reverses the slight, encouraging David to believe that his good reputation holds. "If anyone should rise up to pursue you and to seek your life, . . . the lives of your enemies [God] shall sling out as from the hollow of a sling" (25:29). The sling had been David's weapon against Goliath. Abigail remembers, and she wishes David to know she does.

Throughout the land David is also known as a musician and poet. He is skillful with the lyre and composes many beautiful psalms. Abigail, too, has a literary gift, which she reveals purposefully in her plea, "The life of my lord shall be bound in the bundle of the living[1] under the care of the Lord your God" (1 Samuel 25:29). Abigail could have simply said, "Long live David! God will protect you!" Instead she uses elegant imagery to express God's favor toward him. A "bundle" refers to a sheaf or sheaves of papyrus tied to form a book. "The bundle of the living" is the same as "the book of life." By saying that David's life shall be bound within this bundle, Abigail is assuring him that God will defend him from death. She offers this assurance with a literary flair that reminds David of his own and helps him to recall that he is not a crude, rash, selfishly violent man, but rather a man of God, the Lord's anointed.

Finally, with a prophetic voice that she and David may not even recognize, Abigail proclaims convincingly the very promise of God to David: "Please forgive the trespass of your servant; for the Lord will certainly make my lord a sure house, because my lord is fighting the battles of the Lord; and evil shall not be found in you so long as you live" (1 Samuel 25:28). After King Saul has died, David will establish his own reign in Jerusalem, to be known as the city of David. God will promise to him, through an oracle by the prophet Nathan, not just a glorious kingship but also a dynasty, a *house*. David's sons and their sons shall also be kings, anointed by God, who will establish an everlasting covenant with them:

> I took you from the pasture, from following the
> sheep to be prince over my people Israel; and I
> have been with you wherever you went, and have
> cut off all your enemies from before you; and I will
> make for you a great name, like the name of the
> great ones of the earth. . . . Moreover the LORD
> declares to you that the LORD will make you a
> house. When your days are fulfilled and you lie
> down with your ancestors, I will raise up your off-
> spring after you, who shall come forth from your
> body, and I will establish his kingdom. . . . Your
> house and your kingdom shall be made sure forever
> before me; your throne shall be established forever.
> *2 Samuel 7:8–9, 11–12, 16*

"The LORD will certainly make my lord a sure house," urges Abigail. David has not heard this promise before. But something about Abigail's words, her presence, her conviction, stirs him and renews his faith. He remembers his anointing by the prophet Samuel in the home of his father, Jesse. He remembers that he is God's chosen. Even running for his life, with a band of ravenous, wild men, surely he is God's own.

Abigail does everything in her power to save Nabal's life. Her efforts reveal the depths of her grace. She is, we learn, a theologian, a politician, a poet, a prophet. Bravely, she crosses the boundaries of what her society believes is acceptable for her, a woman, to do. She draws on all her resources, using her beauty, her husband's wealth, her intelligence and wisdom, her rhetorical gifts, her awareness of political events, and her theological insight to make her appeal to David.

At first Abigail succeeds. David is profoundly impressed. "Blessed be the Lord, the God of Israel, who sent you to meet me today! Blessed be your good sense, and blessed be you, who have kept me today from bloodguilt and from avenging myself by my own hand!" (1 Samuel 25:32–33). David accepts Abigail's gift of food and sends her home in peace, promising not to seek revenge against her husband.

Nevertheless, after this momentary answer to her prayer, Abigail loses the life she has known. As Abigail returns to

Nabal, he is hosting the sheepshearing feast and is drunk with wine. She waits until the morning light, then tells him about her experience with David. When Nabal hears the news, his heart dies within him and he becomes like stone. Ten days later God strikes Nabal fully dead.

Those ten days of waiting, of wondering, of hoping must have been agonizing for Abigail. She had come so close to saving Nabal's life. She had convinced the Lord's own anointed, David, not to kill Nabal; surely, then, the Lord was not seeking Nabal's death. Even if Nabal's heart had died, was *he* really dead? Would he yet live? What was this strange death that was not quite death?

As Abigail waited, perhaps at times her hope flourished and in other moments waned. Her waiting and uncertainty, especially about what more she might do to help, must have been exhausting. Did there ever come a moment when she began to view *real* death as a blessing, as some relief from suffering, despite all she would then endure as a widow?

God strikes Nabal dead after ten days. Ten is the sum of two numbers, seven and three,[2] both of which in the Jewish tradition represent wholeness, completeness. By God's act Nabal's death is finally and completely accomplished. Is God punishing Nabal for his arrogant lack of hospitality? Or is God acting in mercy, much like in our own day, when families compassionately decide to end medical life support because life seems no longer to be truly in their loved one who has been so very ill? When God takes Nabal's life, how does Abigail feel about it all?

In the end Abigail saves David, but not her husband, and barely herself.

One could say that Abigail's story has a fortunate ending. Upon hearing of Nabal's death, David sends messengers to ask Abigail to become his wife. She accepts his proposal. Even without the benefit of foreseeing David's glorious future as king, Abigail might favor David as far more interesting, and certainly wiser and kinder, than Nabal.

Yet Abigail does not rejoice. She tells David's messengers that she will come to him as one of the lowliest members of society to do the most menial of tasks. "Your servant is a slave to wash the feet of the servants of my lord" (1 Samuel 25:41). Gone are her wealth and status in society. Before, she had gone out to David with many young male servants and lavish gifts; now, she travels to him riding a humble donkey and bringing only five maids with her. Gone are the young men who had served her. Gone are the sheep and the goats, the feasts, the merrymaking. Whereas Michal, David's first wife, had married him for love (18:20), Abigail, his third wife, marries him in desperation. At least by marrying David she will not have to beg among other widows.

Abigail is, undoubtedly, a widow experiencing profound loss and grief. Her sorrow likely stays with her. Quite soon she will have to flee with David to live among the Philistines, as King Saul renews his campaign to kill David (1 Samuel 27:1–4). Later, when David and his entourage return to their homeland, Abigail, among other Israelite wives, sons, and daughters, will be kidnapped by another enemy, the Amalekites, causing the people to turn against David and seek to stone him (30:1–7).

David will ably defeat the Amalekites, and once King Saul finally dies, establish his reign. Abigail will give birth to David's second son, Chileab. Yet, even after the Lord restores the fortunes of David, Abigail will never be a central and powerful figure, as she was as Nabal's wife. Nor will her son play a major role in Davidic history. As a minor character, he will, like his mother, disappear into obscurity, never to command his father's affection like David's firstborn son, Amnon; his rebellious son, Absalom; and his beloved son, Solomon, who will become king after David.

As Abigail grieves silently, we weep, too. For during a crisis of unstoppable death, we came to admire her. Now, we wonder, does she, in quiet moments of prayer, relive that crisis? Does she ask herself, again and again, whether she could have done anything else to prevent Nabal's death?

☯∿☯

Prayer and Meditation

For Widows
- Remember the hours, the days just after the death. Did you wonder how you might have kept it from happening? What were your feelings?
- Did you tell anyone about your feelings? Did you tell God?
- Do you believe now that it all could have turned out differently? How do you feel?
- Imagine sitting with Abigail at Nabal's bedside after his heart dies.
- Imagine watching at the foot of the cross.

For All
- Ponder those times when you have failed, even when you tried your very best.
- Have you ever felt like you have lost everything? What kept you going?
- Think about the many ways we, in our contemporary world, believe we can prevent death. How do you try?
- Remember that you are dust, and to dust you shall return.

☯∿☯

Anne

I saw it coming. But that doesn't mean I was prepared for it. The day after I finished my last course in spiritual direction at seminary, David started having sharp pains in the middle of his back. We joked that it must be a psychosomatic reaction to my finally finishing my degree. But the pain got worse, until some days he couldn't even make it to work. His internist referred him to a neurologist, an orthopedist, and an endocrinologist. He went to a pain-management specialist, who sent him for physical therapy. He tried a chiropractor and a Chinese acupuncturist. With a psychiatrist he looked into the possibility that his pain really was psychosomatic. All too often he was anxious and I was annoyed. No great fan of doctors, I would grumble to him about this flurry of medical activity and wonder, to myself, whether he might be overreacting. Didn't most people have back pain sometimes?

As months went by, though, his discomfort seemed less and less like most people's back pain. When, despite all the treatments, he constantly needed prescription pain medication and couldn't walk without a cane, the pace of diagnostic testing picked up. By then he couldn't drive, so I took time off of work to accompany him. I sat with him for hours while he waited for blood tests, X-rays, sonograms, CAT scans, PET scans, and MRIs. I gagged sympathetically as he swallowed bottles of radioactive contrast material and winced as he was injected with dyes. Eventually he went to an oncologist for a bone marrow biopsy.

But we still didn't know what was wrong until after the November morning when, more than six months after the pain began, he tried to get out of bed and couldn't control his legs well enough to walk. The emergency medical technicians arrived quickly, decided that his blood pressure was too low to risk a trip to the hospital in Manhattan where his internist was waiting for us, and whisked him off to a neighborhood hospital. There they discovered that he was having severe gastric bleeding from all the pain medications.

While we were waiting for a bed to become available in the intensive care unit, a doctor took me aside and told me that David might have small-cell carcinoma. Small-cell carcinoma is the disease from which his father and brother had died. It is an aggressive form of cancer that is often difficult to diagnose, perhaps because, instead of beginning as one tumor, it scatters itself in tiny clusters at various points in the body. In other words, it is metastatic from the start. And it is incurable.

There are treatments that work for a while, the doctor informed me. People with this type of cancer who receive chemotherapy and radiation often improve quickly and may even feel well enough to return to work. Unfortunately, however, he went on to explain—after pausing to ask me whether

I might wish to sit down—the treatments typically lose their effectiveness, and patients with this disease seldom live longer than about six months. Stalling for time while I located and activated my "I am strong and can cope with anything" mask, I asked him whether he'd discussed this diagnosis with David's internist. He replied that he had; the internist had wondered whether David might want to sign a Do Not Resuscitate (DNR) order.

So we saw it coming. We had time to make choices. The choices David made from that point on amazed me. In dining-room debates over the years, he had crafted eloquent arguments in favor of assisted suicide and "right to die" legislation. He had said often enough that if he couldn't live the life of a reasonably vigorous and healthy person (the "walk and work" test), he didn't suppose he would want to live. But now that he could neither walk nor work, he suddenly seemed willing to do just about anything to keep on living. After his oncologist came to the hospital and presented us with the treatment options, and I'd spent the next half hour wailing, "I just want to be with you!" into what I could reach of my husband's chest around the IV tubes, he started by revoking his DNR order.

I had always thought of him as courageous, but the fortitude he now demonstrated surpassed anything I'd ever seen in anyone. He seemed strengthened and energized by his decision to keep going. His next several weeks were spent in the hospital being blasted with nearly lethal doses of chemotherapy and radiation. He gradually recovered from the gastric hemorrhage while at the same time contending with the side effects of the cancer treatments. When his blood pressure dropped so low one night that his doctor thought it might be time to gather the family, he calmly announced to us that he was not about to die. As soon as the spinal tumor that impeded the use of his legs shrank in response to the treatments, he got a walker and began pushing it one laborious step at a time down the hospital corridor, trailed by a physical therapist and a wheelchair. By the end of the month, he'd recovered enough to come home with me.

If the choices David made surprised me, those I made surprised me almost as much. For decades I had been unrelentingly career-focused. If I missed work for even a day, I was sure I had neglected something essential. Also, I'd always regarded taking care of people as a terrifying burden. Earlier that year, during the months of David's undiagnosed back pain, I had complained in my journal: "What he needs is a wife who is eternally upbeat and cheerful and encouraging. I'm not that wife." I didn't think I had what it took to deal adequately with illness. But suddenly, after not having been to work since the day the ambulance took David to the hospital, I had no interest in returning to my job. If David was determined to live as long as he could, I was determined to support him. With hardly a glance backward, I relinquished my position at the college to stay home with him.

It was a hard, cold winter. Our home is a narrow row house whose three stories are connected by steep flights of stairs, so we had to live in the basement for a few weeks after he left the hospital, until he finally got strong enough to walk up to the main floor and then ride up to our bedroom on a motorized stair climber. Day after day we listened to weather forecasts, alert for storms that might get in the way of our traveling to Manhattan for chemo and radiation treatments or that might strand us once we got there. We struggled with a wheelchair or walker along snowy sidewalks swept by icy winds. Both of us were constantly tired. Both of us began losing weight, he from illness and I from running up and down stairs all day.

But there were good times, too. By February David was able to walk with a cane on his better days, and occasionally he even felt well enough for us to visit a favorite restaurant. He still hoped he might be able to return to work, and so chose not to tell his co-workers he had cancer. Once in a while someone would ask me whether he was a "difficult patient." Although he was known to be cantankerous at times in the face of minor irritations, under these circumstances he proved to be anything but difficult. He was cooperative and appreciative of my caretaking. We became adept at working as a team. Helping him care for his ailing body made me feel at once honored, tender, and protective; it took our relationship to places it had never approached before.

"Restore our fortunes, O LORD, / like the watercourses in the Negeb," I pleaded in the words of Psalm 126 in my morning prayers. I found myself asking God to "just help me get through the next four hours." On occasions when I felt restless or confined by the narrowed focus of my life, I took respites for errands, meals with friends, or meetings with my spiritual director or therapist. I joined a yoga class as a way to take care of my own body and do something new. But mostly I wanted to be with David.

As the doctors had predicted, the improvements eventually eroded. One evening I came home from yoga to find that he had fallen on the living-room floor when his legs abruptly gave out. He began to feel short of breath. He had more trouble getting himself to eat. I don't know that he ever told anyone he realized he was dying. The week before his death, he was still stubbornly undergoing daily radiation treatments. He treated death as an enemy whose nearness he chose not to acknowledge, at least not out loud. But he must have known.

His final trip to the hospital was on Easter Sunday morning, as the bells of the church down the street sang of Christ's Resurrection. He barely made it down the porch steps and into the car, even with the help of his 6'3" son, Josh. My last conversation with him was late the next night, just before he underwent a surgical procedure to drain fluid from his chest. He seemed unusually irritable and distant. When I bent to kiss him before the medical personnel chased me out of the room, he did not meet my eyes. Perhaps by then he was beginning to look toward the place he was going, where I would not be able to go with him.

The following morning I didn't begin the one-hour drive to the hospital until after 9:00 a.m., having arrived home after David's surgery only six or seven hours before. I decided not to call him before I left, supposing that he would still be groggy from the sedatives or would be upset if he couldn't reach the phone. On the way I stopped to pick up something I thought he might be able to eat, because he'd been having trouble swallowing. When I got to his room, his bed was empty. Trying to rein in my dread, I tracked down someone who told me he had just been transferred to the ICU. There

I learned that his breathing had deteriorated so much during the night that he had agreed to go to intensive care and be put on a respirator.

When Josh and I were allowed to see him hours later, he was too heavily sedated to open his eyes or communicate with us. From time to time, as doses of sedation started to wear off, he would become agitated, perhaps from the discomfort of the respirator tube. To see him in that condition, present yet not present, seeming to consist more of machinery and plastic tubing than actual flesh, was disturbing beyond description.

Several years earlier he and I had drawn up living wills and health-care proxy documents. David had designated me to make medical decisions for him if he became unable to do so himself. In his living will, he had stated that "if my condition is terminal and hopeless and death is imminent, . . . I withdraw my actual or implied consent to . . . all further treatment of me by artificial means and devices (such as the use of a respirator)." However, the doctor who had transferred him to the ICU before my arrival informed me that he had been alert and his mental processes had seemed fine when he gave consent for the respirator. In light of the choices he had made about his life over the past few months, his decision to go on a respirator after all did not surprise me. Still, it looked as if eventually the question might be, at what points would he wish to have various types of "artificial means" discontinued?

I sought information about his prognosis from his doctors. At first they thought he might be able to breathe on his own if his collapsed lung were restored to function, so I authorized attempts to do that. Then there was talk of his being able to live on a respirator in a hospice or nursing home. His children and I shared our misgivings about how he would feel about that.

Confused and overwhelmed, I fled to the hospital chapel, pulled a notebook out of my bag, and started scribbling a letter to God. I wrote about what I'd seen, what I felt, what the doctors had said. I begged, as usual, for the strength to get through the next four hours. I pleaded for help in making the decisions David would want me to make. Eventually I wrote that if his oncologist were to tell me the cancer was advancing rapidly, then "I have to help him let go. I have to let him go." An English sea shanty from a record we used to listen to years ago began to play in my head: "Farewell to you, my own true love; I am going far away . . ." I stopped writing in mid-sentence, overcome with the enormity of the loss I was already beginning to experience.

When David's daughter Helayne, a medical doctor, arrived from Rhode Island, his oncologist voiced the opinion that David's deteriorating condition was due to the progress of the cancer. At that point the emphasis shifted to decisions about how to keep him comfortable without unduly prolonging his life. Guided by the oncologist's and Helayne's suggestions about which treatments would have which effects, we increased the sedation, continued the respirator, and withdrew the medication that was supporting his blood pressure. The time to gather the family had come.

Debbie and her husband, Bob, came in from Long Island. Another day went by. When I ventured outside for a break, I found myself rushing from one church to another in that Manhattan neighborhood, draping myself over pew after pew and sobbing out my agony over whether David might have felt abandoned that last morning he'd been conscious and I hadn't been there or phoned to tell him I was on my way. I cried out my grief that he was beyond communicating with me now. "*Please* send an angel to comfort him!" I shrieked at God over and over in my utter helplessness to comfort David myself.

Several times during his last day, it looked as if he might die before his son and daughter from Oregon would be able to get there. But he waited for them. "Judith and Daniel have arrived," I announced to him when they walked into the room. "We're all here with you now." Then each of us spent some time alone with him, saying whatever needed to be said and hoping that he might be able to hear.

At 10:00 p.m. that Easter Thursday, a couple of hours after the sunset that concluded the eight-day festival of Passover, David died, with his three daughters, two sons, first son-in-law, and me circled around him. I hope he was able to see us supporting him and supporting one another as he departed. There were seven of us there with him. *Seven*, the number that in many spiritual traditions signifies wholeness and completion.

A year later I might ask myself, Could I have prevented David's death? The biblical Abigail was able to prevent her husband's death only at first. Ultimately, when Nabal's heart died within him, there was nothing more she could do. Like Abigail, I marshaled my resources, including some I hadn't realized I had, to try to help David stay alive. But I, together with David's mighty will to live and the support of all medicine's horses and all medicine's men and women, couldn't keep him from dying. For me, then, the lingering question is not whether I could have prevented his death, but rather, Did I make the right choices at the right times?

Do I wish I'd done something differently while he was still alive? Of course. I wish I hadn't been so skeptical and cranky during the months before his cancer was diagnosed. I wish I'd stayed by his side every minute and cared for him flawlessly. I wish I'd picked up the phone and called him that last morning before he went to the ICU. I wish I'd said whatever things I never got around to saying while he could still hear them. I wish I'd known for sure what his wishes were about the decisions I had to make as his health-care proxy. In the weeks after his death, I wrote long letters to him, detailing everything I regretted.

But *could* I have done better? In order for me to live with any measure of peace, I have to think of myself as a human being who did the best I could in a complicated, emotionally charged situation. I cannot go back and redo any of it.

Jane

The evening Prosper died, I was angry with him. We argued over a lime-green sweater. I had picked up Whitney, our two-year-old, from day care at the hospital where I worked. We were a bit late getting home. He met us at the door, so glad to see us, and greeted Whitney with his usual exuberance. "Who's that girl? Who's that girl?" She ducked her head, coyly, not looking at him. He scooped her out of her stroller, lifting her high over his head, a big grin on his face. Then, high in the air, she looked down into his face as peals of laughter and chuckling flowed. They loved the game. His usual homecoming ritual.

I was tired; my boss, a gastroenterologist, had seen many patients that day. So, as I stood there, smiling, I was already caught up in the chores to be done and didn't reach out to hug him. He forgot to kiss me. A package had arrived, my new lime-green sweater. Now wearing it, I asked if he liked it. He commented that it looked a bit snug. Hurt, I slipped into angry silence. Though I suspected it was tight, I liked the way it looked.

It was a muggy evening in early May. "Should I go to my meeting or should I go for a run?" Pros was a recovering alcoholic with five years of sobriety. Tuesday night was his lawyers' AA group. "Go run," I said, "you always enjoy it." I turned away, impatient. There was dinner to cook and clean up, homework, baths, and bedtime stories.

Later, sometime around 7:00 p.m. I am told, he collapsed while jogging on the Brooklyn Bridge, as his family ate dinner, expecting him to arrive home any minute. "Don't wait dinner for me," he had called out as he closed the door, "I'll eat when I get home." As I prepared the uninspired meal, I thought, "not worth coming home to." Pros was an excellent cook, a gourmet. His meals looked good on the plate and tasted heavenly. I cooked out of necessity, to feed the body. Pros fed the soul as well as the body with his meals. So that night it was to be the mundanely prepared bluefish, which he had insisted on rushing over to Court Street to buy during the day, although he sounded tired over the phone. He had been irritable for two days. And tired for several months. More than should be normal, he often napped in the evening. He was not himself. Also, his complexion was gray, not his usual ruddy glow. But I didn't know.

If I had known, could I have done anything to stop the ending of his life on this earth on that muggy May evening in 1988?

The minutes ticked by as the girls chattered and we ate our

dinner. I bathed the little one, read her a story, and carried her off to bed. As the little body next to me relaxed into sleep, in the quiet dark I began to feel a growing sense of unease. Something was not right. He had gone out about 6:00 p.m. He should have been home within an hour, but it was now after 8:00 p.m. In the rush of evening chores, feeding the children and getting them to bed, I had forgotten about him. I forgot, forgive me, I forgot. A terrible dread stole over me, filling my heart with darkness, freezing my limbs, numbing my mind. "He should have been home by now," the dark whispered. I remember that I cried out, an inarticulate prayer to God for help. Gradually, almost miraculously, a calm came over me, a purpose, and a knowledge of what to do. I calmly went in to Jordan, our sweet but very savvy ten-year-old. She was watching television. "Daddy isn't home yet; I am going to run next door to the church and tell my prayer group friends that I will be late." She barely glanced at me. Thank God for television, that enemy of all "progressive" parents in the 1980s, along with refined sugar and Barbie dolls! I was suddenly grateful for the mind-numbing banality of television.

When I ran into the church, I allowed myself some panic, "Something is wrong," I cried out, "Pros is not home yet." Hurried explanations ensued, and my friends said soothing things. They decided to go home with me. We told Jordan that we had decided to hold prayer group at our house. I calmly got her into bed. Then I began to telephone the hospitals, the police. Finally, around 10:30 p.m., a return call from the police: "Mrs. Parkerton, they have someone at Beekman Downtown that might fit the description of your husband. But we need more information. A car is coming over right now." I should have known then, but my mind was feeding me only the bits of truth I could handle.

The two young policemen who came to my door were so nice, suggesting that perhaps I should go down to Beekman myself and see if it was my husband. "Is he okay?" I asked. They said they didn't know. They did a good job in their role. I was going to rush to the hospital on my own, but they gently insisted that someone should go with me. One friend stayed with the girls, and two others went with me. Did my friends suspect he was already dead? Most likely. I never asked them.

As my friend drove us over the Brooklyn Bridge, Pros's bridge, I remember thinking that he must have been mugged, knocked unconscious. How else to explain his apparent inability to tell them who he was? I thought of how I would scold him, gently, of course, our clash over the lime-green sweater faded from memory. I would hug him and tell him that he scared me so. Perhaps I would miss a day of work. I hoped he wasn't badly hurt.

But somewhere deep inside my heart, a small voice warned that this night would not be easy.

It wasn't until we reached the emergency room that I realized the two young policemen had followed in their car. As we rushed inside, I was actually smiling in anticipation. I couldn't wait to hug him and make the evening all right. But the place was so big, the lights were glaring, and no one seemed to know where he was. The two policemen had a hushed conversation and then conferred in more hushed tones with some nurses and doctors, while I kept scanning the room looking for a stretcher with my husband on it. Finally a nurse led us into a small cramped room. The dread was slowly seeping in; something was not right.

A weary doctor began to speak in a hoarse monotone. At first I couldn't grasp what he was saying. It was something about finding a man on the bridge and trying to revive him. The ambulance brought him here, and they spent another twenty minutes trying to resuscitate him. At that point my growing panic exploded in rage, and I yelled, "Are you trying to tell me that my husband is dead?!" The doctor continued without once looking at me, his "if it is your husband" the only acknowledgment of a truth that was beginning to lodge in my heart and mind as reality.

At that moment, when the ground opened up to swallow me, my priest arrived. I threw myself into his arms; he comforted me. He took over. Told me not to worry. He'd take care of things. Told me I didn't want to see the body. I didn't? Or did I? In time I would regret not seeing Pros's body. I

wished I had said good-bye. But in that moment, I felt res-
cued, saved, taken care of.

Later, many regrets and questions plagued me, "Why
didn't I insist on seeing him one last time?" being only the
first. The question that woke me up many nights to come,
stopped me dead on streets with tears streaming down my
face, broke my heart, gave me no peace was: If I had said to
Pros, go to your meeting, and he had gone, would he still be
alive today? Would the clot, or the arrhythmia, or whatever
it was that caused his heart to stop, have passed harmlessly
through without the added stress of jogging? Or would someone at his meeting have been able to perform CPR? His
friends would have caringly shepherded him to the closest
emergency room. "Call 911—Pros is down—he's still breathing—I've got a heartbeat—hold on Pros, you'll be okay, just
hang in there, buddy." But he was among strangers, on his
favorite bridge, on a muggy evening in May. And I was home
struggling to get a mediocre dinner on the table and help
with homework. And nursing resentment about a tight-fit-
ting lime-green sweater.

He was dead almost instantly, the ER nurse told me. "His
big heart just burst!" she said. I hope this is true. I hope he
didn't suffer or spend his last moments on this earth worrying
about us, his family, and how we would manage. But even
now, sixteen years later, I can still sob my regret as I write
this: What if I had not been angry with him, what if I had
been paying attention, to him, to his needs, to his appearance over the past few days, that he looked gray and pasty-
faced, that he complained of being very tired? What if I had
insisted that he see a doctor? But I was not thinking of him.
He slipped through the spaces in my heart given over to children, daily chores, and myself. When he died did he say, "Tell
my wife I love her"? or "Tell my wife that running on the
Brooklyn Bridge is the way I would choose to go"? or "Tell my
wife I love the way her sweater hugs her voluptuous curves"?
Maybe. I will never know.

chapter two

Naomi

Ruth 1:1–22

She wishes to change her name. No longer call me *Pleasant,* she tells the women of Bethlehem. I am not the same woman you once knew. Call me *Bitter.*

Naomi, whose name means "pleasant," has become the most imperiled kind of widow. Her husband and only two sons have died. She is too old, she believes, to remarry. In Bethlehem, her parents are no longer living, and because she has lived abroad in the country of Moab, she is unsure about how her other relatives may react to her return home. When she left with her husband for Moab years before, Bethlehem had been suffering a severe famine, which is why they had taken the risk of moving to a sometimes hostile neighboring country. Recently, she had heard that the Lord, out of consideration for her people, had ended the famine, yet she does not know for certain that she will find food to eat.

Naomi's loss is staggering. She has no husband, children, home, food, or decent clothes. She is likely very hungry, exhausted from her journey, and frightened. How humiliating it must be for her to return to the town of her childhood as a poor widow, looking decades older than she did when she left.

As soon as she arrives in Bethlehem, the whole town is stirred, and her friends, women she had known as a child, who may have been bridesmaids at her wedding or wet nurses for her sons, come to greet her. "Is this Naomi?" they ask, stunned.

Naomi's first words to the women reveal the depths of her plight and despair. "Call me no longer Naomi, / call me Mara," a name that means "bitter," "for the Almighty has dealt bitterly with me" (Ruth 1:20).

In this poignant moment, Naomi is being completely honest about her feelings. Seeing her friends, who still have husbands, children, and homes, who have not lost everything, and who bear such compassionate looks of shock and concern, Naomi undoubtedly feels resentment. Why are they better off? What has she done to deserve her fate?

And yet, with her close women friends, Naomi may also find a freedom to express her profound anguish. Before, in Moab, among a foreign people, she may have always felt the need to be guarded. Similarly, on the return journey to Bethlehem, she may have felt she had to show courage. Traveling with her two Moabite daughters-in-law, Ruth and Orpah, she had begun to show her feelings, weeping aloud with them. "The hand of the LORD has turned against me" (Ruth 1:13). But she also may have felt a responsibility, for their sake, to be strong. "Go back each of you to your mother's house," Naomi urged them, sacrificing the comfort of their companionship. She kissed them farewell. "May the Lord deal kindly with you, as you have dealt with the dead and with me. The Lord grant that you may find security, each of you in the house of your husband" (1:8–9). Orpah had agreed, but Ruth had insisted on remaining by her side. "Where you go, I will go," Ruth vowed (1:16). When Naomi realized she could not persuade Ruth to return to Moab, she spoke no more to Ruth. As they traveled on, she fell into stoic silence. She kept her sorrow to herself. It is only with the women of Bethlehem that Naomi's despair again bursts forth.

Call me *Bitter*. Naomi's words are even more astonishing to the women of Bethlehem than they are to us, because we, today, are less culturally aware of the power of names. People in the Bible understood that an individual's name does more than simply identify the person. The name also reveals the essence, or inner reality, of the individual, as well as the person's place in history and community. Biblical families, therefore, took great care in naming their children. A name, moreover, helps to build relationships. In *Naming the Mystery*, Episcopal theologian James E. Griffis writes:

> When two friends who have known one another for many years and shared much together use each other's names, the name refers to a history of involvement and love as well as a knowledge of the other person—what he or she likes and dislikes, feels and thinks about many things, believes about his or her place in the world. A name can carry with it a knowledge of another person that is deeper than one person can express directly about another; it carries with it a history of feelings and shared memories that language cannot express.[1]

When Naomi tells the women of Bethlehem to call her by a different name, she is saying that she is no longer the friend they knew. Her essence has changed; she is different, unrecognizable. She feels very alone.

Even more striking for the women is that Naomi takes it upon herself to try to change her own name.[2] To do so is unheard of, because only God has that kind of authority. In Naomi's day, no one other than God could rightly change a person's name, because doing so would reveal the power of, and command a new allegiance to, the one making the change.[3] In the history of God's saving acts, God had changed Abram's name to Abraham (see Genesis 17:5), Sarai's name to Sarah (see 17:15), and Jacob's name to Israel (see 32:28), attesting to God's power and the faithfulness those ancestors were to offer God. Astoundingly, Naomi, a woman and a poor widow, is trying to usurp God's power.

Does Naomi realize what she is doing? Perhaps not, as her grief is so overwhelming. Her words might simply be a desperate reach for some sense of control when she feels so helpless. She has no power over anything, least of all death. But at least she can wrest control over her name.

Or perhaps Naomi is candidly expressing defiant anger to her friends. She may no longer be willing to offer any allegiance to God. God did this to me, she might be confessing to her women friends, so I will serve only myself now. God will no longer have power over *me.*

Or she may view a change in her name as what God actually intends for her, because she believes God has brought her affliction upon her.

> I went away full,
>> but the Lord has brought me back empty;
> why call me Naomi
>> when the Lord has dealt harshly with me,
>> and the Almighty has brought calamity
>> upon me?
> *Ruth 1:21*

That is, by causing her situation, and the emotional changes within her, *God* is changing her name, even if she is the one to call for the name change aloud. Call me Mara, for this is God's will.

Naomi might even be saying all these things. Are not they all various facets of grief—reeling helplessness, anger, acceptance?

What is remarkable about Naomi's story is that no one ever does call her Mara. Deep down, despite everything, she will be Naomi. She will be herself, even if she cannot, in the throes of acute grief, feel like herself.

In the midst of her anguish, Naomi's friends see who she really is. They know her by name. They love her. And they offer her a safe place to express her every emotion. They listen to the raw, unprocessed, *unpleasant* feelings of early grief.

For widows, then, Naomi reveals the rightness of expressing difficult feelings, no matter how foreign they seem and how frightening they are. Widows can be bitter, angry, or sad, especially among people they trust, without losing themselves. Widows may pray, and share with others, all that is in their hearts.

Naomi's story also encourages those of us who befriend widows not to offer superficial comfort, try to stop their weeping, or demand their strength and courage. Death is rough, and cannot be expected to be otherwise. Rather, we do best to walk with widows in their pain, as Ruth did, and to listen graciously to their hard feelings, as the women of Bethlehem did. Most of all, we are to assure them, again and again, no matter what has happened and no matter how much they feel changed into something horrible that they do not recognize, they are still themselves, remembered and beloved.

❊

Prayer and Meditation

For Widows
- When you ponder your loved one's death, are you ever angry or bitter? If so, do you seem like yourself or a stranger?
- Do you ever get angry with your friends?
- Are you able to tell anyone when you hurt?
- Pray Psalm 77:1–10. Observe a brief silence. Then, from the beginning, pray the entire Psalm. Tell God which part of the Psalm seems most true.

For All
- Have you ever returned to your childhood home? What was that like?
- Have you ever changed your name or wished to? Invite God to remember with you.
- When you become angry or bitter, how do you then let go of those feelings? Is it easy or difficult?
- Into a quiet place, take with you something that has a bitter flavor, such as one of the bitter herbs, or *Maror*, traditionally used in Passover seders—raw horseradish, romaine lettuce, or chicory. Settle yourself, then slowly eat. Pray for God to be present with anyone who may, in this moment, feel like the food tastes.

❊

Anne

In the days after David died, I had trouble figuring out how to interact with people. I felt dazed and delicate. Everything irritated me. I found it difficult to focus my attention on anything other than the events surrounding David's death, which kept replaying endlessly in my head. Whatever I was feeling seemed enormous and barely comprehensible.

The week after the funeral, dozens of people came to our home to pay condolence calls, including friends and colleagues I hadn't seen in quite some time. "Oh, Anne . . . how *are* you?" many of them asked as they stepped into the living room, their faces alight with looks of compassion, curiosity, sorrow, or trepidation. "Uh . . . well, I . . . uh . . . okay" I would mumble in response, my own face undoubtedly alight with a look of confusion. I knew these people cared about me, and I knew I felt dreadful. But how could I put that feeling into words? I also knew my clothes were two sizes too big, I had dark shadows under my eyes, and I looked drawn and ill without my customary makeup. What answer could they possibly be expecting?

During that period I spent a lot of time with my friend Judy, for whom the landscape of bereavement had become familiar, having lost both of her parents within the past couple of years. She provided immediate guidance about the Jewish practice of sitting *shivah* after the funeral, and served as an understanding presence afterward. At one point we exchanged e-mails about problematic things people say during condolence calls. She recounted how some of her family's visitors had talked on and on about how shocked they were when her mother or father died (after years of decline from cancer or Parkinson's disease). Other visitors had described in distressing detail their own relatives' deaths.

"Not many people recounted their relatives' demises or told me how they felt when they heard the news," I replied to Judy. "But they did ask a question that had me completely stumped." Then I listed the possible replies that had gone through my mind when people asked me how I was:

Question: *How are you?*
Answer 1:   *Fine, thank you. How are you?*
Answer 2:   *Miserable, thank you. How are you?*
Answer 3:   *My one true love just died. How the hell do you suppose I am?*
Answer 4:   *Take a good look at me and see if you can guess.*
Answer 5:   *How would you feel in this situation?*
Answer 6:   *Shitty. Just shitty.*
Answer 7:   *What do you expect me to say to a question like that?*
Answer 8:   *What answer would make you feel most comfortable?*
Answer 9:   *Exhilarated, because now I can finally tell you the truth about what happened.* (David had concealed the nature of his illness from most people.)
Answer 10: *Like I'm underwater. Everything seems slightly distorted.*
Answer 11: *Abandoned. David's kids had to go back to their regular lives, my relatives weren't well enough to travel here, and his other relatives didn't come to the house.*
Answer 12: *Never mind that. How did you feel when you heard the news?*
Answer 13: *Overwhelmed. I have no idea what I'm going to do with all this rotting fruit.* (I had a lot more refreshments than visitors.)
Answer 14: *Uneasy. What do I know about sitting shivah? I'm trying to do the right thing here, but what if I do something that makes David the laughing stock of Judaism?*
Answer 15: *Relieved. Now I'm not sick with worry about whether he's in pain or frightened or being neglected in the hospital, or whether he'll have an awful death like his brother had.*
Answer 16: *Like somebody died.*

As soon as I saw these imagined responses on my computer screen, I realized that some of them sounded sarcastic or hostile. The people who asked how I was had taken the trouble to visit and make an effort to comfort me, and for that I was grateful. They were voicing their concern and sympathy in the best way they knew how. "How are you?" is a common social expression, not necessarily a question that demands an answer. Besides, I was never sure what to say when I made condolence calls, either. So why the angry responses?

One afternoon, while Judy and I were sitting at my dining-room table trying to eat up the leftover fruit, it occurred to me that my frustration with the question may have arisen in part because I was having so much trouble expressing my grief and articulating my needs to other people.

Privately I cried every day. I cried many times every day. I wrote letters to David, put them in my loose-leaf journal, and cried. I wrote letters to God, put those in my journal, and cried some more. I set up pictures of David all over the house and bleated at them, over and over again, "Where *are* you?" and "Please come *baaack!*" I stood at his dresser and sobbed into the threadbare green V-neck sweater he'd worn all winter to his radiation and chemo treatments. But my friends and relatives rarely saw or heard any hint of these intense feelings. What they saw and heard instead was my Okay Act.

Over the course of my life I'd developed considerable skill at acting as if I were absolutely on top of things, no matter what. "Oh, yeah, I'm doing okay!" I would reassure my parents whenever I called them after David died. My sister was contending with a medical problem that soon would result in the amputation of her leg; our eighty-five-year-old parents were doing their best to help her, and I was not about to bother any of them with my problems. "Oh, well, it's kind of hard, but I'm definitely getting there!" I would tell a former co-worker brightly when she called to ask how I was faring. A couple of my friends did have a clearer idea of how bad I was feeling because I told them about it in e-mails, but even they seldom, if ever, saw evidence of it in person. What they got when I was with them was my Okay Act. The main person with whom I had always been able to set aside the Okay Act was David. Unfortunately, he was dead now.

In many circumstances, "acting okay" can be a valuable

social skill. But as the months after David's death went by, I continued to hide my grief even in those situations where sharing it might have comforted me or made me feel less alone. Instead, it would pop up in inconvenient or unhelpful places. I almost never cried in my therapist's office, but I'd be blinded by tears when I walked into the drugstore where I used to get David's medications. I would sound just fine in our Ruth and Naomi Circle at Grace Church, but I had to start avoiding certain grocery store aisles because seeing my husband's favorite foods could easily trigger a crying jag. When with friends, I could discuss all manner of things about his death in a rational, composed way. But driving on the highway alone one day, I nearly got into an accident when a song on the radio made me sob so hard I felt like I was being turned inside out. My Okay Act gave people the impression that I was coping remarkably well and so did not need any special help. Why, I wonder, was it—and is it—so hard for me to let other people see my grief?

"People used to wear black for a full year when somebody in their family had died. Everyone could tell at a glance that they were bereaved, and could make allowances for them," observes Barbara Cawthorne Crafton in *The Sewing Room:* "We don't do that today. . . . We paper over our heartaches after a week or two, and everyone around us soon forgets we had them."[4] The distinctive mourning garb must have been helpful to all concerned. However, I am not so sure that "everyone forgets." Perhaps everyone would *like* to forget. After David died, some people, including a few who had been my friends for many years, seemed to be avoiding me. After the initial rush of funeral attendance and condolence messages, I rarely heard from most of the people at the school where David and I had worked for more than thirty years and whom we had thought of as our second family. I've been told that some former colleagues speak of me almost as if I, too, had died ("Oh, she was so nice . . ."). This past Christmas, my first without David, I was dropped from some of our friends' holiday card lists. Even at church most people never acknowledged my loss. It is hard not to notice that my situation tends to generate avoidance.

"Is this *Naomi?*" the biblical widow's former neighbors exclaim in astonishment when she returns, wretched and bereft, to her hometown. At times I have felt as bitter as Naomi. One thing that takes some of the edge off the bitterness is to try to understand people's reactions. Though it is true that I didn't show a great deal of initiative in keeping in touch with people after David died, I also suspect that people may remember all too well the cause of my heartache and are further reminded of it whenever they think of me. Perhaps that is part of the problem: my grief, my loss, may make the prospect of dealing with me just too uncomfortable. It is painful to be close to it. And it reminds us all of an aspect of life we cannot control but ultimately will not be able to avoid.

I haven't felt a lot of external pressure to "paper over" my heartache (probably because my Okay Act does such a good wallpaper job already). But as the first anniversary of David's death approached, I worried about what might happen next. Even if I had been wearing black for a year, the year would soon be over. What if I continued to feel wounded and off balance? What if my Okay Act chose that point to desert me? Although I tend not to ask people to make allowances for me, it was reassuring to know I could and people would understand. Once the first year of mourning was over, would anybody cut me any slack if I needed it?

Jane

My father died very recently, leaving my mother a widow after fifty-nine years of marriage. During a troubled time when I was a young adolescent, I remember debating within myself, nights before I fell asleep, the question, "If you had to lose one parent, which one could you give up?" It wasn't a matter of which parent I loved more, for I loved them both as much as any child can. Rather, it was which, my mother or my father, was more essential to my well-being, to my sense of home. Which one could I afford to lose if I had to choose? I never reached a satisfactory conclusion, but time decided for me. On May 30, 2004, my father died in his sleep, having just turned eighty. Yes, he was sick; he was experiencing increasing difficulty breathing with lungs scarred from rheumatoid arthritis and complicated by a heart weakened from lack of oxygen. And yes, it was sudden and unexpected, as death always is when it comes to take those we love.

So my brother, sister, and I are left with the care of our mother. Mama at eighty-five is deaf. Her body is bent with arthritis and frail from malnourishment. Yet she is surprisingly agile. It is her mind that is failing her; she has some form of dementia as yet undiagnosed. She has refused to leave the house for years, especially to go to a doctor.

During the first week after my father died, I stayed with my mother, sharing her sadness and an occasional laugh or light moment. One lucid afternoon, she said sadly as she gazed out the window: "I don't know what I will do without Willie around. This is not home anymore." But in the past few months, their house had more frequently not been home to her. Her confusion had worsened to the extent that she sometimes even forgot who my father was. And she had begun increasingly to beg, bargain, and plead to be taken "home."

My mother would pack, unpack, and repack her bags, and we would sit and wait, wait for "Papa" to come and get her. For she meant to return home to her mama and papa. Never mind that the home she remembers is not there anymore. My grandparents died when I was a teenager; my mother was a young woman. The house and farm were sold; the trees were cut down for lumber. The house has been replaced with cornfields. The forest she roamed, the fields her father planted, even the country roads are completely unrecognizable. The landscape has changed too much.

The biblical writer tells us that Naomi has lost her husband and two sons. The home that she and Elimelech had made in the country of Moab suddenly is not home anymore. Naomi determines to return to the land of Judah, her childhood home.

When my husband died, unlike Naomi, I remained in the alien land that my husband and I called home, raising our daughters in the same apartment we moved into when we were first married. My family assumed that I, now a bereft widow alone with two small children, would want to return to Tennessee, to the place and people of my childhood. But "home," I had come to understand, is not a place so much as it is people. The community my husband and I had become a part of, in our sixteen years of marriage, was and is now my home.

My sister, Kris, also spent time with Mama, before my brother, Will, found a suitable nursing home. My mother continued to plead to be taken home. At one point, when Kris's reserves were sitting on empty, when she was exhausted from a day of explaining every fifteen minutes who had died and where she was when it happened, my mother said, "I wish Papa would hurry and come get me." Seeing my mother's frailty and clutched with fear for the future, for Mama's future, Kris whispered, "I do too, Mama; oh, God, I do too."

Waiting for Papa

Jeweled tears reflect deep sadness in my mother's eyes
"Did someone die?" she inquires of the room.
"Daddy—your husband—died, in his bed, here at home."
She sunk back into her chair her body bent with time and disease
"Papa's coming," she said, "Papa's coming to take me home."

Kissing her cheek, I offer, "I love you, Mama."
She turns to me, smiling graciously, "I don't know you very well
but . . . I feel we have a connection."
Returning to my chair, I sit to wait with her and wonder,
Does God drive a team of mules hitched to an old farm wagon?

chapter three

❈

The Widow of Zarephath

1 Kings 17:8–24

SHE IS A WIDOW WITH A YOUNG CHILD. He is a son, thank goodness, who offers her hope for the future. Her son is the heir to
her husband's estate. Because of him she will be able
to remain in the two-story house left behind by her husband.
In her old age, her son will care for her, and she will not have
to beg for provision, like many of the widows without sons in
her society. With love for her child, therefore, and because of
the promise of her future sustained in him, she strives fiercely
now to care for him. Nevertheless the drought is severe. She
has only enough coarsely ground grain for one more supper.
After they eat this last meal, she realizes, they both will die.

We might be surprised to find the widow of Zarephath's
story in the Bible, because she is a foreigner. She lives in a
Phoenician town on the coast of the Mediterranean Sea,
south of Sidon. This is the land of Baal, Asherah (also
known as Astarte, "the goddess of the Sidonians" [1 Kings
11:33]), and other pagan deities of the Phoenicians' polythe-
istic religion. These gods do not have the same compassion
for the poor as does the God of Israel, who is "Father of
orphans and protector of widows" (Psalm 68:5). A righteous,
or Torah, society under God's command is to care for widows,
for example, by leaving the gleanings of harvest and vintage
for poor widows to gather for food. Compared with an
Israelite widow, therefore, a Phoenician widow is of even

lower estate and more precarious position. For the widow of Zarephath, there is no one to offer protection and security except her son.

The setting for her story is the reign of Ahab soon after the united kingdom of David and Solomon splits into two, a southern kingdom called Judah and a northern kingdom called Israel. As ruler of the northern kingdom, Ahab sets about pursuing evil and offending God. He marries Jezebel, a Phoenician princess from Sidon, near where the widow of Zarephath lives. In the northern kingdom's most prominent city, Samaria, he builds a house and altar to Baal, as well as an *asherah*, a sacred pole that is the symbol of the goddess Asherah. By marrying a foreign wife and worshiping foreign gods, Ahab does "more to provoke the anger of the LORD, the God of Israel, than had all the kings of Israel who were before him" (1 Kings 16:33). Jezebel, meanwhile, is also incurring God's wrath; she has been murdering the prophets of God (18:4,13), even as she invites the prophets of Baal and Asherah to feast at her table (18:19).

Into this troubling situation comes Elijah, whose first prophetic act is to stand before King Ahab and proclaim a drought that will not end except by Elijah's word. It is this drought, and the resulting famine throughout the lands of both the Israelites and the Phoenicians, that is causing the widow of Zarephath to struggle to feed her son.

After leaving Ahab, Elijah goes into seclusion at the Wadi Cherith, where ravens feed him during the time of want. But soon the wadi runs dry, and the word of the Lord comes to Elijah, "Go now to Zarephath, which belongs to Sidon, and live there; for I have commanded a widow there to feed you" (1 Kings 17:9). Elijah sets out and finds the widow gathering sticks for a fire. He asks at first for a little water. Then, as she is going for the water, he calls out to her, "Bring me a morsel of bread in your hand" (17:11). After many days of hunger and desperation, and with not enough food to share, the widow protests that Elijah's request is more than she can bear. "As the LORD your God lives, I have nothing baked, only a handful of meal in a jar, and a little oil in a jug; I am now gathering a couple of sticks, so that I may go home and

prepare it for myself and my son, that we may eat it, and die"
(17:12).

That we may eat it, and die. The widow's candor is disturbing, and her words take us aback. Yet we are also astonished
at the widow's persistence. For even when she believes she
and her son cannot possibly carry on, when food and hope
are gone, when death seems the only outcome left, the
widow still wishes to prepare a last meal. She will do what
she has always done before, every day of her son's life. She
will attend to his daily need for food, protection, comfort,
love. Despite all.

Her faithfulness to her son must touch Elijah's heart,
because he urges the widow not to be afraid. Her jar of meal
will not be emptied, he promises, and her jug of oil will not
go dry. Go ahead, he encourages, include me in the meal. You
will never starve, even as long as the famine endures. When
the widow does as Elijah requests, the jar is never emptied of
grain and the jug never runs dry of oil. Elijah stays with the
widow and her son many days, sharing meals with them,
growing in friendship with them.

It is a miracle of daily provision, reminiscent of God's provision of manna centuries before when the people of God
wandered in the wilderness after their escape from slavery in
Egypt. The manna had been like dew from heaven, with the
appearance and taste of coriander seed, and the people had
ground it and prepared it as cakes whose taste was like that of
cakes baked with oil (see Numbers 11:7–8), much like the
meals the widow prepares for herself, Elijah, and her son.
Perhaps during their meals together, Elijah tells the widow
and her son the story of the manna. Perhaps the widow tells
stories, too, about the boy's father, about how much her son
reminds her of him.

In some sense Elijah offers to the widow a companionship
she had lost. One purpose of marriage, according to the
Episcopal liturgy for the Celebration and Blessing of a
Marriage, is to provide "the help and comfort given one
another in prosperity and adversity."[1] Because of the death of
her husband, the widow of Zarephath has no one to help and
comfort her in a time of severe hardship. Yet God sends to

her Elijah. He is not her husband, nor will he become her
husband, yet he is, for a time, her *companion*, a word whose
meaning is, literally, "with bread." Elijah shares bread with
her, sustaining her through a time of trial.

One day, however, the widow's son becomes very ill, and
his breath departs from him. Holding her son to her bosom,
with tremendous grief, she lashes out at the best friend she
has, Elijah: "What have you against me, O man of God? You
have come to me to bring my sin to remembrance, and to
cause the death of my son!" (1 Kings 17:18). Overcome with
despair, the widow reveals the depths of her feelings to the
one person she trusts not to turn away, even when she blames
him, as she also blames herself, for her son's death.

Once again, as he has every day before, Elijah renews the
widow's hope when all seems hopeless. Taking her son's body
to the upper room of the house, he prays fervently to God,
then stretches himself upon the child, in a strange and holy
ritual, to restore the child to health and return him to his
mother. Like the jar that is not emptied and the jug that does
not run dry, the revival of the widow's son is a miracle of provision, of life, hope, and future.

One can interpret the story of the widow of Zarephath as
a polemical argument for the supremacy of God over Baal,
Asherah, and other gods worshiped by the Phoenicians. It is
telling to compare the fates of the widow of Zarephath and
Jezebel, the wife of King Ahab, both from Phoenicia. The
widow is in one of the lowliest positions of Phoenician society, while Jezebel is a Phoenician princess. The widow keeps
alive Elijah, a prophet of the God of Israel, whereas Jezebel
slays hundreds of prophets faithful to God. Through her
friendship with Elijah, the widow comes to know that "the
word of the Lord in [Elijah's] mouth is truth" (1 Kings 17:24).
Her relationship with Elijah offers her conversion. By contrast, Jezebel never converts, even after her marriage to King
Ahab. She continues to worship the Phoenician gods and
persuades her husband, King Ahab, to do so. In the end, the
widow's son lives, and she lives, not as an outcast widow, but
as a mother in the home of her son. The same blessed fate is
not Jezebel's. Because of Jezebel's "many whoredoms and

sorceries" (2 Kings 9:22), she and her son Joram die horrible deaths. Joram's heart is pierced by an arrow in battle, and his body is thrown to the ground to decay (see 9:21–26). Soon after, Jezebel is thrown out of a window by two of her own eunuchs. She is trampled by horses, after which her dead flesh is eaten by dogs (see 9:30–37).

Yet the story of the widow of Zarephath is more than simply a persuasive narrative revealing God's triumph over foreign gods. It is also a stirring account of how a widow, even in the pangs of grief and even in the most difficult of circumstances, can both care for others and discover hope for the future. For the widow of Zarephath, hope is manifest both in the life of her son and in her relationship with Elijah, her companion.

As her son grows into adulthood, we wonder whether she will tell him about the sources of her hope. Will they tell family stories about the time of famine and their friend Elijah from abroad who stayed with them? Will she confess to her son that, on one very frightening day, he died, and that Elijah, by prayer and faith in God, had restored him to life? Will she call this a miracle? Or will she worry that, if she does tell him, her son might ask why his father could not also be raised from the dead? Will she wonder about this, herself? Will she be able to trust that all shall be well, regardless, because her husband lives on in her son?

⊙⌒◎

Prayer and Meditation

For Widows
- Do you have children? Is that helpful, or does it hurt?
- If you do have children, do they remind you of your loved one? What is that like?
- Tell God how you feel about the future.

For All
- Have you ever cared for someone when all seemed hopeless?
- Jesus taught that we must become like children to enter

the reign of God. What does this means to you, given
our mortality?
- Imagine holding the baby Jesus in your arms.

ⓞⱾⱾⓞ

Jane

"You can't make a promise like that. You might die tomor-
row!" My small but fierce ten-year-old daughter, Jordan,
flung those words at me in fury in the hours after Prosper, my
husband and her father, died. Putting my arms around her, I
had whispered, "Don't be afraid Jordan, I will never leave
you." I was trying to comfort her—and myself as well, I must
honestly say. Oh, foolish grown-up! Even a child, most especially Jordan, saw the emptiness of that promise. It isn't likely
I will outlive her. Some day I, too, will die and leave her. As
we had just so tragically learned, someone you love and
depend on can die in an instant.

"It's Whitney I feel sorry for the most, Mom," she said. "She
doesn't have the memories." But even memories proved cold
comfort in the face of daily life without Pros. After he died,
the children cried some, but not often, not what you might
expect. Whitney was so young and didn't really understand.
For a long time, she later told me, she thought her daddy was
living in the basement. As long as Jordan and I were there
and her routine was the same, Whitney seemed fine, even
with a bizarre daddy who lived in the basement. And Jordan,
for the most part, carried her grief and loss inside.

I am the one who mourned openly, shedding freely my
tears and words of loss. Then the girls would rush to comfort,
wrapping small arms around me, and cry, too. Once some
well-meaning adult said, "You should stay strong, for the children." Not grieve or cry in front of them, she meant. What
she did not understand, but my daughters did, is that my
mourning served us all. Whitney didn't yet have the words,
and Jordan was too much like her father; she kept her feelings inside until she sorted them out. So when I cried and
mourned, we all cried, and we told the stories, stories that
kept him alive in our midst and shaped our daily life.

We carried on. Once a family of four—father, mother, two little girls—we were reduced in a heartbeat to three bewildered females. And I, I was Mom, single parent, "head of household," according to the government. I kissed all scraped knees and bruised psyches. And I feared the day when a kiss would be so woefully inadequate to ease the hurts of life.

About four months after Pros died, as she was falling asleep, Whitney asked me, "Did my daddy's body die?" "Yes," I answered, "your daddy's body died." There was a silence. Then she said, "Where is my daddy's face?"

Ah yes, her daddy's face—a bigger, stronger version of her own—large hazel eyes, long lashes, and a smile so wide and warm that it filled your heart to bursting. It was his smile I fell in love with before I even got to know him. Just one month before her third birthday, what was Whitney asking? "Yes, your daddy's face died. But his love didn't. He still loves you."

"It's not enough," Jordan said. She was telling me about what her dad said and did when he put her to bed. He always held her hands, his big hands folded in prayer around hers, and together they would say the Our Father. Then he often would lie down next to her and fall asleep. She could even mimic his snores. Remembering those moments, she paused and said, "All we have left are memories, and that is not enough."

We talked of him frequently and observed his birthday, the anniversary of his death, and all holidays faithfully. We kept him alive and with us with our words, and I with my tears. And my daughters felt secure because, in spite of my tears and grief, I took care of them. I was there, day after day. Meals, homework, schedules, visits to Grandma in Connecticut, and annual trips to Tennessee all happened as usual. We remained in our home; we went to school and church and work as usual. Routines did not change immediately after his death, but only slowly, as we grew and changed.

When the teen years arrived, I alone waited up nights for a wayward daughter to return, lecturing and yelling and crying about curfews and responsibility, while she yelled back, or worse yet, smiled and hugged me. "Sorry, Mom," came the automatic response while the excitement and freedom of the illicit night winked gleefully in her smile, in the pitying look, in the whiff of cigarette smoke.

I could stay up half the night after they were in bed, sobbing and raving at God, reading Job and writing letters to Pros, but the next morning I had to be up making breakfast and getting us out the door to start a new day. The daily challenges and crises of life with children had to be met. Lunch money, permission slips, and bruised egos. Dinner and homework. Brownie meetings and Easter bunnies. Halloween costumes and carving pumpkins. Santa and putting up the Christmas tree. Red geraniums for the gravestone. I might cower and tremble at night in my bed, but the next day I was on! That's what having children demands of you. Two little people whom we, in our innocent passion, brought into this world now depended on me, and me alone. I could bend, but I couldn't break. I could tremble in fear of what disaster might overtake me, but I couldn't quit. I could shake my fist in fury at God, but ultimately all I had was God and Pros's children. Without them I would have been truly alone. With them I had hope. Without the children I cannot imagine what I would have done. Through them he lived and continues to live. Because of them I had to get up in the morning, cope, do well. I had to live and love and laugh again, so together we could envision our future.

On Thursday, May 12, 1988, two days after her father died, Jordan wrote this poem:

> Tragidy marks the spot
> Don't plan that terrible plot
> As terrible as I feel
> It will take some time
> For the sadness to heel.

Yes, it has taken a long time for the sadness to heal, for the memories to bring comfort as well as tears. Our girls are grown now. Some say they look like me, but they both are exactly like him. Jordan has his sharp, analytical mind, his preciseness, and his dexterity with his hands. She has his sense of humor. Whitney does look like him; she has his smile and his eyes, but she also has his easygoing disposition. Are they scarred? Probably. But, then, how many of us escape scars in life? Truthfully, would we want to? For I do believe that, because of all that has gone before, they have grown into capable, confident, courageous, and loving young women—daughters to be proud of.

Anne

When David died, he had three daughters, two sons, and four granddaughters. He was predeceased by another son, who was killed in an automobile accident more than thirty years before. But I did not give birth to any of his offspring, nor to anyone else's. David's children are adults now, with careers, families, and homes of their own. As their father's third wife, I was not part of their lives until they were in their teens and twenties, and I was in my thirties. I probably seemed to them more like an older sister or a young aunt, the latest to be grafted onto a family whose genogram resembles a complex wiring diagram.

David often marveled at how well his children turned out, as if that were some extravagant, miraculous gift he hadn't earned. He was right to marvel at them; they all are, in their own individual ways, the kind of talented, capable, good people any parent would be proud of. I cherish my relationships with them and their spouses and children. I am delighted by the ways they remind me of their father. And the sight of his blue eyes sparkling in his granddaughters' faces often brings tears to mine. During those last hours with David, I thanked him for the wonderful family he had brought into my life.

So I can only imagine what it must be like to be left with children to raise. I do not have to worry about how to carry out the fearsome responsibility of nurturing and supporting young lives without the help of a mate. I do not have to worry about how to comfort grieving children. I have no one whose life depends on me. I am free to remake my own life however I see fit.

But this coin has another side. In *For Those We Love But See No Longer: Daily Offices for Times of Grief*, Lisa Belcher

Hamilton revealed: "When my husband died, I wanted to die too. It helped to have a little boy with soft baby skin who needed me, only me, to nurse him."[2] I can understand the wish to die, and I can imagine the salvific effect of the baby with his unique and absolute need for his mother. Especially in the early months of acute, aching grief, it must be helpful to have someone for whom to go on living.

Many times since David died, I have thought the ancient Hindu practice of being a *sati* (a true or virtuous wife), a widow who throws herself onto her husband's funeral pyre, makes a lot of sense. I miss David and want to be with him. It is difficult to contemplate a future without him, with all its uncertainties and the prospect of more caretaking and bereavement as my parents age. There seems precious little to keep me here. I have no children to protect. And there is no one to protect me.

At the moment, my mother and father are in good health for people in their mid-eighties. That is fortunate, because they spend much of their energy caring for my sister, who is in her early fifties and has disabilities. There are no other relatives. If I eventually become the only able-bodied person among them, I will have to watch more loved ones become sick and die. If I get a serious illness such as cancer, who will take care of me the way I took care of David? At times I am terrified. Caretaking is hard, and loss is painful. If David were here, we could face those challenges together. If I had had children, they would be old enough now to be able to help and comfort me. Without David and without children of my own, I sometimes worry that my future might turn out to be more than I can bear.

Natalie and Joyce are former co-workers of mine whose husbands also died, Natalie's a few years ago and Joyce's a couple of months after David's death. Natalie has four grown children, and Joyce has two.

"What did you do about Joel's clothes?" I asked Natalie as she was showing me around her redecorated apartment.

"Oh, I had the kids come over and take care of them. I went out for the afternoon, and by the time I got back, everything was all packed up and gone."

"What are you going to do about getting a headstone for Phil's grave?" I queried over a cup of tea at Joyce's dining-room table.

"Oh, my son and daughter are taking me to a monument place next month. My daughter got a recommendation."

Oh. Oops. If I had asked David's children to help me with such tasks, I'm sure they would have. Before she left after the funeral, for instance, one of his daughters asked if I would like her to take away his clothes, but at that point I wasn't ready to have her pack up anything except his medical equipment and all other evidence of his illness. Since then I haven't thought to ask for help. My counterdependent Okay Act is, I'm sure, one reason. In addition, I am not David's children's mother; they have living mothers who are not me. Does that make me imagine I am not entitled to their help now that their father is gone?

The story of the widow of Zarephath is about spectacular miracles. A desperate woman who is about to die of starvation suddenly finds she has plenty of food; when her son stops breathing, someone brings him back to life. I suspect that any miracles that might occur in my world will be nowhere near as obvious. Chances are I will have to play an active part in making them happen—and perhaps I'll have to look carefully in order to recognize them at all.

These days my fears about the future hurt so much that I am trying to focus on the present and, as they say in twelve-step recovery programs, to let go and let God. What I am trying to remember is that I need to entrust my life, and my anxiety about it, to a higher power. I need to remember that it is not all up to me. I need to learn how to ask people for help and how to accept help when it is offered. I need to remember how, four hours at a time, I managed to accompany David as he journeyed toward death. Most of all, I need to remember that God might also get me through whatever further trials and losses my future holds.

Maybe that can be my hope for the future. Maybe that will be a miracle.

chapter four

The Widow with Two Coins

Mark 12:38–44, Luke 21:1–4

SHE CATCHES JESUS' ATTENTION. All day he has been in the Jerusalem Temple teaching spellbound crowds and disputing with hostile religious authorities. Perhaps he is tired, for now he takes a moment to sit opposite the Temple treasury. He is in the Court of the Women, an area of the Temple beyond the Court of the Gentiles, where foreigners may visit, but before the inner rooms into which only Jewish men may enter. Within the Court of the Women are thirteen trumpet-shaped chests in which people may place their financial offerings. Each chest is for a special purpose, such as to collect the Temple tax or money for the purchase of doves, incense, or wood for the ritual sacrifices. As Jesus pauses, he watches people, rich and poor, placing money into the treasury. The rich are giving large sums. The widow enters and offers two small Greek coins, each called a *leptos*, which literally means "small or thin one." The *leptos* is the smallest of all coins. The widow's contribution touches Jesus, and he calls his disciples to witness her giving. "Truly I tell you, this poor widow has put in more than all those who are contributing to the treasury. For all of them have contributed out of their abundance; but she out of her poverty has put in everything she had, all she had to live on" (Mark 12:43–44).

How does Jesus know the two coins are all the widow has?

For centuries Christians have interpreted the widow's story as a model of sacrificial giving and absolute dependence on God. In that view, the poor widow gives into the treasury generously and faithfully. She offers her very life, symbolized by the two small coins, trusting that God will yet provide for her. In the Episcopal Church's calendar of Sunday readings, her story is paired with the one about the widow of Zarephath, who also shows complete faith in God by feeding the prophet Elijah with the only food she has left in a time of drought (see 1 Kings 17:8–24). The sacrifices of these two widows foreshadow Jesus' own sacrifice, and abandonment to God, on the cross. Therefore, as Christians we are to make similar sacrifices, relinquishing our need for security, wealth, and status and trusting not in our own self-provision but rather in God's steadfast love and care. As a small measure of our faithfulness, we are to be generous, like the poor widow, in making financial gifts to our parishes, our contemporary version of the Jerusalem Temple.

To wonder how Jesus knew the depth of the widow's poverty, however, is to begin to see her story within its broader narrative context and to explore a different interpretation of the story and its meaning for us.

Jesus seems already to know the poor widow. As he watches her, Jesus is aware that she is a widow, although he may recognize this simply by widow's clothing she might be wearing. More impressively, Jesus also knows that she has no resources left at all. How?

A few days before, Jesus had made a triumphal entry into Jerusalem, with crowds of people spreading cloaks and leafy branches along the road before him and shouting with joy, "Hosanna! Blessed is the one who comes in the name of the Lord!" (Mark 11:9). The crowd's enthusiastic response to Jesus raised fear and anger among the religious authorities. Then, on Jesus' first day of teaching in the Temple, he began to drive out merchants who were selling and buying and to overturn the tables of money changers. God's house, Jesus proclaimed, "shall be called a house of prayer for all the nations. . . . But you have made it a den of robbers" (11:17).

Jesus' fierce action increased the ire of the religious leaders, who then began to seek a way to arrest and kill him.

Did Jesus meet the poor widow on that first day in the Jerusalem Temple? Had she been begging near or within the Court of the Gentiles, where the money changers worked and where she would encounter the most people? Is that how she came upon the two small Greek coins? Perhaps Jesus spoke with her and learned her history. Perhaps his conversation with her, and others like her, so enraged him that, swept by emotion and the Holy Spirit, he began to cleanse the Temple, literally, of economic injustice.

As he teaches in the Temple before his death, Jesus focuses on the injustices of the Temple's economic life. Unfairly, the Temple's religious authorities are serving their own economic interests. An excessive burden of taxes and financial offerings required for proper worship and for ongoing construction and renovation of the Temple is causing poor peasants to sell their lands and other property and sometimes even their own children into indentured servitude. Both with direct teaching and in parables, notably the parable of the wicked tenants, Jesus harshly condemns the corruption within the Temple economy. The crowds are delighted, and the religious authorities are outraged.

In Jesus' teaching, widows represent all the very poor. "Beware of the scribes, who like to walk around in long robes, and to be greeted with respect in the marketplaces, and to have the best seats in the synagogues and places of honor at banquets! They devour widows' houses and for the sake of appearance say long prayers," Jesus preaches in the Temple. "They will receive the greater condemnation" (Mark 12:38–40). Jesus' intimate familiarity with the Hebrew Scriptures may inspire him to use widows, in his preaching, as representative of all who are oppressed by the Temple's overbearing economic demands. Often in the Scriptures, Jesus knows, widows are a symbol of unjust economic practices that evoke God's wrath. Yet, as he preaches, Jesus may also be remembering the poor widow who gave her last two coins, and other real widows, whose histories and situations grieve him.

When Jesus calls his disciples to come and see the poor widow giving her last two small coins into the Temple treasury, therefore, he may not so much be praising her selfless dedication and generosity as challenging economic injustice.[1] Most of the trumpetlike chests within the Court of the Women are not for voluntary donations, but rather for offerings legally required for worship. Had the poor widow begged for the two coins so that she could begin to fulfill her religious obligation? Is Jesus revealing the horrific consequences of a Temple economy that steals the life of the poor?

According to Mark's Gospel, Jesus' observation of the poor widow's offering is his very last act in the Temple. Never to return, he will go forth toward the cross proclaiming the Temple's impending destruction. As Jesus departs from the Temple with his disciples, one of them will admire its grand architecture. Jesus will retort, "Do you see these great buildings? Not one stone will be left here upon another; all will be thrown down" (Mark 13:2). Some years later the Romans will indeed destroy the Temple, and Jesus' disciples, inspired to lead a new kind of life, will create an alternative economic system that will care for the poor. In the early Church, no one will claim private ownership, and everything owned will be held in common. Those who are wealthy will sell what they own and lay their offerings at the feet of the apostles, who will distribute the gifts so that no one will be in need (see Acts 4:32:35). Within this new economy, widows, particularly those who have no other financial resources, will receive appropriate care and provision (see Acts 6:1–6, 1 Timothy 5:3–16).

For our own spiritual growth, we might do well to embrace both interpretations of the poor widow's story. Such is the mystery of Jesus' teaching, which often imparts more than one idea. The widow who gives her last two coins into the Temple treasury might be for Jesus, and for us, both an exemplar of selfless giving *and* a manifestation of the urgent need for a just economy.

Certainly, by teaching and example, Jesus does urge us to make willing and loving sacrifices. Because we follow Jesus, we yearn to be deeply sacrificial as we give to others and to God, in order that we might approach Jesus' own self-offering. We might reflect, therefore, on what "deeply sacrificial" looks like in our own lives. For widows who may feel as though they have already sacrificed so much, and who realistically may have much less to offer financially, emotionally, or otherwise since their loved one's death, Jesus' call to sacrifice may be especially difficult to understand, accept, or continue answering. Perhaps the poor widow with two coins also struggled with Jesus' teaching.

Surely, also, Jesus exhorts us to care and advocate for those at the economic margins of our society. Just as Jesus shared table fellowship with, offered comfort and healing to, and prophetically called for the forgiveness and embrace of outcasts and sinners, so must we.

To be faithful followers of Jesus, then, we need to be both generous and just. Individually, are we? As participants in our economy? How about as members of social institutions, such as the Church? As a holy temple built of "living stones" (1 Peter 2:5), are we, the Church, faithful to God's intentions for us?

Do we give of ourselves *and* work for justice, with all that we are and all that we have, honoring all people?

❧❧❧

Prayer and Meditation

For Widows
- Who handled the money before your loved one died? Who manages your financial affairs now?
- Is death expensive? In what ways?
- Do you worry about money?
- Does being a widow change your understanding of what sacrifice is?
- Does God provide?
- Offer a candid prayer to God about a current financial need or desire.

For All
- Are you scared you will not have enough money?

- How generous are you with money? If you have ever lost income, did your generosity change?
- When Jesus condemns the rich, what are your emotions?
- Confess to God about a time you felt financially uncharitable.
- Do you trust the Church to care for the poor?
- Put two pennies in your pocket. To the next person who begs of you, give the two pennies. Then, tell God how you feel.

๏๛๏

Jane

One of the most pressing questions confronting me after my husband died was how to survive financially. Prosper was an attorney, so one might think we would be financially secure. Such was not the case. About four years prior to his death, he quit his comfortable government position to enter private practice. A year and five months before his death, I returned to work as an administrative assistant in a medical department at a nearby hospital—and only at his urging.

Pros's reasoning was that we needed the protection of the benefits, especially health insurance, that a full-time job would provide. As a newly established sole practitioner, he could not afford the cost of private insurance for himself and his family. I remember only that I resented deeply the pressure on me and felt acutely the wrenching pain of leaving our year-old daughter, Whitney, my baby, in day care.

In retrospect, his insistence that I get a full-time job was just one of his judgment calls for which I grew to be grateful. Another that stands out and serves us still was his insistence that we rent the apartment that has served as our family home for thirty years. When we moved to Brooklyn Heights, we found two apartments that could be our future home. Both were garden apartments. One was smaller, darker, and in a brownstone whose owner occupied the other floors; the other was rent-stabilized and more spacious, with its garden open on all sides to light and air, and with Grace Church as a neighbor. I wanted the smaller, darker apartment because it had two working fireplaces. "Those are coal-burning fire-places!" Pros exclaimed in exasperation. Eventually, I bowed to his reason. I have never regretted it. His wisdom and fore-sight continue to provide for us.

I cannot imagine how difficult it would have been for me to look for a job in those weeks and months after Pros died. As it was, I had been employed at the hospital just long enough to establish a place for myself, and I was able to take time off to grieve and, later, to work with only a small frac-tion of myself focused on the job. My supervisor and co-workers were understanding and supportive. Because the hospital was only two blocks from where we lived and eight blocks from where my daughters went to public school, I was readily available to run out if the school or day-care center called. My oldest daughter, Jordan, who was ten when Pros died, found it very reassuring to know I could get to her within minutes of a telephone call.

So with my salary and my husband's Social Security bene-fits, we were able to remain in our rent-stabilized apartment. We developed a routine to accommodate our new status as a mother and daughters without a husband and father. I dropped off and picked up Whitney from day care; Jordan was invited to a neighbor's house after school.

And money, which had always seemed in short supply while Pros was alive, suddenly seemed abundant! Some checks were still coming in for cases he had worked on. A friend paid a credit card bill. Contributions were donated to Grace Church for my children: "Here, this was left for you." "Who?" I would ask. "Anonymous" would be the answer. For the first time in my life, I felt almost rich! So the immediate financial needs seemed covered.

Still, that gave me little comfort. It was the future that frightened me and kept me awake many nights, tossing and turning and worrying. So it is in my continuing relationship with money. I always have the fear of not having enough at some point in the future. I am often anxious even in the midst of abundance.

During my early childhood, my family moved around a lot. My father had difficulty finding employment to support his growing family; he was going to school on the GI bill and working odd jobs. We moved often in search of better jobs and opportunities, back and forth across the country three times (to Oregon twice and Idaho once), from Tennessee to Kentucky twice and back, and within our hometown in Tennessee too many times to count. I changed schools at least once a year.

As a widow with two young daughters to raise, I was often filled with dread of what financial ruin the future might bring. Sure, we had enough to live on, even to enjoy some of the luxuries Pros never felt we could afford. But what about college! When I found out that the Social Security payments for each daughter would end just as she prepared to go off to college, I was paralyzed with panic. My husband's life insurance policy was just enough, just exactly enough, to pay his taxes.

As Jordan grew closer to eighteen and the dreaded day when the Social Security benefit for her would cease, we realized that a small bank account had been growing. Oh, it had been there all along, funded by the initial anonymous contributions, checks from cases Pros had worked on, and tax refunds; it is just that we began to realize that it might be possible, after all, for Jordan to go to college. After a final hellish year of SATs, college applications, sleepless nights, frequent arguments, and countless financial aid forms, Bard College offered her a financial aid package that made it all work. She was launched into life! Was I relieved? Somewhat and not really.

Then there was Whitney. She was ten at the time Jordan went off to school. I knew the next eight years would speedily pass, and there would be no more savings account. Except, there was! The year Jordan graduated from Bard with a BA in fine arts and Whitney entered high school, their grandmother, Pros's mother, died and left them each a small inheritance, enough to see Whitney through two or three years of college. In Whitney's second year of high school, she was accepted into the newly created Bard High School Early College program, a collaboration between Bard College, a small liberal-arts college upstate, and the New York City

Board of Education—public college with a private school education. She will graduate with a high school diploma and an associate's degree. As I write this, Whitney is preparing to go to Guilford College, a small Quaker liberal-arts college in North Carolina, to continue her education.

Our life together as mother and daughters has been blessed with God's abundance, in the goodness and kindness of family, friends, and strangers, and in the continuing financial support of their father. Throughout our journey together, through all the crises big and small, we have always had just enough, just exactly enough. What more can anyone ask?

As I look back over the past sixteen years and meditate on the biblical widow who gave her last two coins, I find myself asking if I, too, have faith enough in all this abundance to give my all. My last two coins—probably not. I am still working out my conflicted relationship with money. But as a parent, yes. For it seems to me that parenting, especially parenting alone, faithfully giving your all each day to your children, including your sleepless nights and panic and tears and fear and laughter and love, is sacrificial giving. Daily I have given my all so that my children can grow into the abundant life God has promised. Truly it has been a most blessed journey.

Anne

Measured against the standards of most of the world, I am unspeakably wealthy. Day after day I have a roof over my head, plenty to eat, more clothing than I need, access to excellent health care, and the resources to heat my home, drive a car, connect my computer to the Internet, go on retreats, and give gifts. Now I even have the luxury of being semiretired.

That said, it's a good thing I worked all those years.

When I was in college, my goals were to get married and get into graduate school by the time I completed my degree. After failing to achieve either goal according to my time-table, I happened upon a temporary job as a counselor at a community college in Brooklyn, hundreds of miles from where I grew up. The job worked out so well that I persuaded the administration to let me continue beyond the six months for which I'd originally been hired. Eventually I got into graduate school. David and I met and got married. I earned tenure and ended up remaining at the college for over thirty years.

Eventually, when I became a spiritual director and felt called to devote more time to that ministry, I left my full-time position and took a part-time job at the same college. Despite the reduction in my income (I wasn't being paid for spiritual direction), we still had David's salary and medical coverage. We didn't miss the money as much as we'd expected. After several more years, I quit working at the college altogether to care for David during his final illness. Even with this further substantial decrease in our income, his sick-leave pay supported us, and his health insurance continued to help with his enormous medical expenses.

Then he died. The paychecks stopped coming in, and our medical coverage terminated the next day.

Not yet old enough to qualify for Social Security or Medicare or to withdraw money from our Individual Retirement Accounts without penalty, I was thankful that I had my own retirement benefits and retiree health insurance to activate.

Now, for the first time in decades, I am not collecting a paycheck, either mine or my husband's. A paycheck, I have discovered, feels quite different than a distribution from a retirement fund. Paychecks are money coming in that wasn't there before. Distributions are money going out that was there before but won't be anymore. My retirement payments are serving as a monthly reminder that my financial resources are finite. I try not to focus too much on the future, but if I happen to live as long as my parents, who are thirty years older than I am, I wonder whether there will be enough money to support myself and whoever else in my family might need my assistance. For the time being, therefore, I'm seeing how low I can keep the payout.

I think people's perceptions of how well off they are financially are highly subjective, influenced by their personalities, their experiences, and, especially, who is around them. I worked at a community college and sometimes volunteered at an agency for displaced homemakers. After a typical week of hearing students and clients tell me about not having enough money to take the subway to school or buy food for their families, I would feel obscenely rich. Now, as a spiritual director and a member of Grace Church, I spend a lot of time with people who can easily afford elaborate vacations, second homes, and private schools for their children. Among them I feel like a pauper. There are days when I think I ought to go back to the community college or the displaced homemakers agency in order to regain some perspective.

Sometimes I wonder what my life would be like now if I hadn't had a steady, full-time job with which to build up financial security over so many years, or if I had children to support or if David hadn't had adequate health-care coverage. Our medical insurance required so much paperwork that I sometimes complained that filing, tracking, and appealing claims was a full-time job in itself, but in the long run it reimbursed us for a substantial portion of the bills related to his illness.

We didn't purchase life insurance because his retirement plan was supposed to pay out the accumulated funds as a death benefit if he died before retirement. As the anniversary of his death approached, however, I had to apply for an extension on his estate's tax return because I was still unable to find out when that payment would arrive or even how much the amount might be. Whenever I call the retirement program administrators these days, I feel like the importunate widow in Luke 18:1–8 ("this widow keeps bothering me"). What do widows in similar situations live on if they don't have jobs or other sources of income?

The delay in the death benefit payment affects David's children as well. Because I am not their mother, he and I agreed that he should not leave all his assets to me, as spouses with children together often do. In his will he provided for his children as well as for me—but until the death benefit check comes in, there is no money in the estate to give them. It is just lucky that none of them is in great need of that legacy at the moment.

I also wonder what I would be going through now if I hadn't been the one who managed our household's finances all along. When I was growing up, my father, who worked in a bank, taught me to balance checkbooks, prepare tax returns, budget resources, and make investments. I've always enjoyed those tasks, and David was glad to have me take care of them. Single until I was thirty-one, I had established credit in my own name by the time we got married. Now, serving as executor of David's will and handling my finances under these new circumstances, I'm sure I would be having more difficulty without this previous history.

Writing about the story of the widow's coins, an anonymous author in *Forward Day by Day* suggests: "It is easy to give when we have an abundance. It is when we have to give up something in order to give that we can begin to understand what it is to feel truly rich."[2] I'm not sure we invariably find it easy to give even from abundance, but charitable giving these days certainly does have a different feel for me. The initial payout I elected from my pension plan, I have discovered, rarely covers even my routine monthly expenses. Whenever I give away money now, therefore, I have to draw upon my savings. In order to give anything, I have to give up a measure of security. But the fact that I am still in a position to give at all does tend to make me feel rich. And lately I have noticed that I'm giving away a greater proportion of my resources than ever before.

Over and over I have said "I was lucky" or "I am fortunate." I was, and I am. I was married to a man who thought it important that I be decently provided for. I was able to work steadily, manage money effectively, and learn to exercise reasonable control over my spending impulses. I probably could get another job if I had to. Although my current financial situation is not as it was when David was alive, I have resources to draw upon and, at present, only myself to support. Frankly, I have not yet come to trust that God will provide for me if I run out of money—so I am hoping to develop more trust before I get down to my last two coins.

chapter five

❧

Tamar

Genesis 38:1–26

SHE FEELS DISGRACED WITHIN HER COMMUNITY. She becomes a widow not once, but twice, after the deaths of both her first and second husbands. Her father-in-law, a man of questionable morality, breaks a promise to her, trapping her in widowhood and leaving her childless. To overcome her embarrassing and desperate situation, she resolves to become pregnant by prostituting herself and tricking her father-in-law into committing incest with her.

Yet, in the end, her shame will turn to honor. She will be praised by her people for preserving the seed of Abraham and helping to fulfill God's promise to the patriarchs of children as numerous as the stars. Her son Perez will become a forebear of King David and Jesus.

Tamar's story begins when Judah, one of the twelve sons of Jacob, leaves his family and goes to live in a foreign land. Already we know that Judah is not trustworthy. He had been one of the villainous brothers who plotted against Jacob's favorite son, Joseph; when the jealous brothers sought to kill Joseph, Judah suggested they instead sell Joseph into slavery, for then the brothers could profit financially (see Genesis 37:26–28). Soon after Joseph disappears, Judah moves away and settles in Canaan, where he marries a foreign wife.

Judah and his wife have three sons, Er, Onan, and Shelah. The eldest son, Er, marries Tamar. Er is a wicked man in the sight of God, and God strikes him dead. Judah then tells his middle son, Onan, to enter into a Levirate marriage with Tamar. When a man died childless, the custom was for his brother to marry the widow in order to produce a son and heir, ensuring that the dead man's name would "not be blotted out of Israel" (Deuteronomy 25:6). Onan, however, greedily refuses to raise up a son in Er's name, presumably because the son would then have a share in the inheritance of Judah's property. Whenever Onan has sex with Tamar, he spills his semen onto the ground. Onan's disloyalty displeases God, and God puts Onan to death. Tamar is now twice a widow.

Judah must now arrange a Levirate marriage between Tamar and his youngest son, Shelah. Judah is afraid, however, that Shelah, too, will die. So he tells Tamar that Shelah is still too young to marry. "Remain a widow in your father's house until my son Shelah grows up," he vaguely promises Tamar (Genesis 38:11). So Tamar must return to her childhood home, trapped in her widowhood. She is betrothed to Shelah and cannot marry anyone else. Because Judah has no intention of allowing her to marry Shelah, she is forced to remain a widow. Her shame burns. Not only is she a widow, but also she is deemed cursed by God, a danger to any future husband.

Once back in her father's home, Tamar is neither a virgin nor a wife nor a mother, any of which would be a position of respect within her society. She remains a widow.

And she continues to wear her widow's clothing, for years.

Perhaps, in her grief, she has neither the desire nor the energy to dress differently.

Perhaps her widow's clothes offer her some sense of identity and belonging, even if only as a lowly widow. Without this sense of self and place within her society, she might be at a complete loss. In her widow's garments, she is at least someone, a widow. Even if she is only on the fringe of her community, she still belongs to Er, her first husband.

Perhaps, also, her widow's clothing serves to remind Judah of his promise.

In the course of time, feeling lied to and disowned, Tamar finally finds the inner strength to change her circumstances. She will take care of herself. In so doing she will be faithful to her dead husband and to God.

Tamar is told that Judah is traveling to Timnah for the sheepshearing. Judah's wife has recently died, and his time of mourning has just ended. Changing out of her widow's garments, Tamar dresses herself in a veil, hiding her face, and sits down at the entrance to Enaim, which is on the road to Timnah, awaiting Judah's arrival.

When Judah sees Tamar, he does not recognize her and believes her to be a prostitute. He approaches her with interest, and she asks what he will pay her. He promises her a kid from his flock, but she demands his signet seal, the cord from which the seal hung, and his staff—all of which can identify him—as a pledge. He agrees, they have sex, and Tamar becomes pregnant. Once Judah departs, Tamar puts back on her widow's clothing.

When Judah sends his friend Hirah with the kid as payment to recover the pledge, Hirah cannot find the prostitute. To avoid embarrassing Judah, Hirah asks the townspeople of Enaim if they have seen the temple prostitute who had been by the wayside. Judah had believed she was a *zonah*, or ordinary harlot, but Hirah describes her as a *kedeshah*, or temple prostitute. In Canaanite religion, cultic prostitution was a common aspect of the worship of fertility goddesses. The prostitutes often veiled themselves, as Tamar did, in order for worshipers to believe they were sleeping with the goddess. To have sex with a temple prostitute would be acceptable in the eyes of Judah's Canaanite neighbors.

The townspeople, however, have not seen the prostitute. Upon Hirah's return empty-handed, Judah, who was so willing for Tamar to live in shame, now seeks to avoid shame himself. He tells Hirah not to worry about exchanging the kid for his signet, cord, and staff. "Let her keep the things as her own, otherwise we will be laughed at" (Genesis 38:23).

Three months later Tamar's pregnancy begins to show, and Judah is irate, believing that Tamar has committed adultery by sleeping with a man other than Shelah. Judah condemns her to be burned, a very harsh sentence. Usually the punishment for adultery was stoning. Judah's condemnation reveals that he, like Tamar, is suddenly burning with embarrassment.

Tamar is bravely ready. As she is brought out to be put to death, she sends word to Judah: "It was the owner of these who made me pregnant. . . . Take note, please, whose these are, the signet and the cord and the staff" (Genesis 38:25).

It is the moment of greatest humiliation for both Tamar and Judah. Tamar is a widow, bereft, shunned by her husband's family. She has tricked her father-in-law and prostituted herself. She is an unwed mother who is being brought out to be burned for adultery. Judah, meanwhile, has not fulfilled his obligation to his son's widow. He has lied to Tamar and broken a promise. He has slept willingly with someone he thought was a prostitute—if a simple harlot, a socially embarrassing act; if a Canaanite temple prostitute, an act of apostasy against the God of his ancestors. Now, on top of everything else, Tamar and Judah are known to have slept together, father-in-law with daughter-in-law, in an act of incest that has led to a pregnancy.

Yet the moment is also a turning point.

For Judah comes conversion. "She is more in the right than I," Judah confesses, "since I did not give her to my son Shelah" (Genesis 38:26). After this, Judah will begin to redeem himself from his shameful past. He will bring Tamar into his household, caring for her as she gives birth to and raises twin boys, Perez and Zerah. Never again will he sleep with her. Soon, he will reconcile with his brothers and travel with them, during a time of famine, to Egypt to purchase grain for their father, Jacob's, household. In a second trip to Egypt, when Joseph, not yet recognized by his brothers, seeks to hold back the youngest son, Benjamin, beloved of their father, it is Judah who will plead for Benjamin's release and offer himself in Benjamin's place. "Now, therefore, please let your servant remain as a slave to my lord in place of the boy; and let the boy go back with his brothers. For how can I go back to my father if the boy is not with me? I fear to see the suffering that would come upon my father" (44:33–34). Judah's plea will so touch the heart of Joseph that, weeping loudly, he will finally reveal himself to his brothers in a tender, compassionate reconciliation.

For Tamar comes salvation. No longer will she live as a childless widow, embarrassed, despairing. No longer will she fear. Her humiliation will turn into honor, her disgrace into grace. She will be remembered with praise for having preserved the lineage of Abraham. Elders will use her name in blessings. To Boaz, the great-grandfather of King David, the elders will say, "May your house be like the house of Perez, whom Tamar bore to Judah" (Ruth 4:12). Tamar, herself, will even be named in the biblical genealogies of King David and Jesus.

Tamar's story reveals the inner strength and resourcefulness widows must find in creating a new life when their helpmate dies, and how difficult doing so can be within a society, both hers and our own, that tends to view widowhood as something shameful. Tamar discovered that she could, with creativity, determination, and courage, take care of herself. The discovery took some time, as it does for many widows. Yet, eventually, Tamar knew she could risk her reputation and her life to give birth to something new. Despite all, she lifted her head and walked into her future.

☉〜◉

Prayer and Meditation

For Widows
- How long does widowhood last?
- Does the loss ever get easier?
- Do you ever feel ashamed of being a widow?
- Tell God what has required your greatest strength and resiliency.
- Remembering the past and embracing the present, pray Psalm 31:1–5.

For All
- Is there anything in your life for which you waited years?
- Have you ever felt like you were prostituting yourself?
- Has anyone ever broken a promise to you?
- Have you ever broken a promise? Seek God's forgiveness.

☉〜◉

Jane

The summer of 2004, the seventeenth summer after Prosper's death, has been a season of loss for me. I am once more facing life alone. Only this time around, I feel more alone than ever.

I have essentially lost both my parents. My father died this past spring, just two months after his eightieth birthday. And my mother's mind has slowly succumbed to a disease that has robbed her of herself, stolen my childhood memories, and taken her to a place I do not know, where I can only trust that God abides with her.

We (my daughters, son-in-law, and I) had just arrived to spend a week vacationing with our Tennessee family. My children stayed with my brother and his family. I planned to sleep at my parents' house, but first, I needed to clean.

A meticulous housekeeper, my mother would never have tolerated the sight that greeted my eyes when I walked through the door. Dirty dishes were piled on every available space in the kitchen; cobwebs swung from the ceilings; grime encrusted the floors and carpets. Now she sat in her old worn armchair, blankly staring out a window while the life she had carefully nurtured and cherished disintegrated around her.

So I, channeling my mother's outrage and shame, spent the last afternoon of my father's life on this earth washing dirty dishes. He died that night, in his sleep. Dear God, where were you? Couldn't you have stopped me from cleaning, told me I could have loved my parents more by sitting at his side that afternoon? We could have talked, my father and I, shared memories and the overwhelming sadness that filled our hearts. Perhaps he would have spoken of one of his most recent "projects"—more grapevines to plant, a new tomato bed to dig, a new floor for my sister's kitchen. What would we have said to each other? What have I lost?

My mother is now living in the Alzheimer's unit of a small nursing home about thirty minutes away from my brother's house. He visits her regularly. Sometimes she knows him, sometimes not. There are so many gaps, so many holes in her memory. Jane, Kris, and Will could be her children, but maybe her siblings? She isn't sure.

My sister and I find this loss in some ways more heart-breaking than our father's death. My brother, with gentle equanimity, is able to meet my mother where she is, enjoying her sweet graciousness and patiently reminding her when she forgets that he is her son, her baby, her last little chicken to leave the nest. Although he has admitted recently that he dreads the day when he no longer will see a light of welcome and recognition in her face when he comes to visit. So I mourn them both, my father and my mother. And cry out to God: "Why? Why couldn't you at least leave my mother her memories?"

More than this, I have also said good-bye to my daughters' childhoods. (At least I *remember* them; I pray that I always will.) I have said good-bye to that intense period of nurturing two young souls who, though deeply loved and loving, struggled from the moment they were born to be separate and independent.

Whitney, my baby, left for college last month. At age seven she would collapse in tears if anyone even suggested she would one day leave home; at age ten she thought she would live down the street. Later, she considered the possibility that a nearby town might perhaps be close enough to Mom. At nineteen, however, she has chosen to attend Guilford College—a small liberal-arts school in Greensboro, North Carolina, and a *very* long drive from home.

Jordan, my firstborn, married Benjamin last September at Grace Church. They are now living in their own home in Lansdale, Pennsylvania. My daughter has chosen well. From the day I met Benjamin, I knew him to be a "keeper"; he is a steady presence to Jordan's passionate spirit. In each other they have found a soul mate, a companion to share the journey.

Alone now in my newly spacious apartment, I sometimes pause to touch the photographs of my little colt-like daughters, stroking their innocent small faces and feeling the pain of loss for the days when I, Mommy, fulfilled all their needs. When Whitney called last week to croak, "Mom, I'm sick—what should I take—could you send some vitamins?" I almost wept for joy, and trotted happily to the store and post office to Priority Mail vitamins packed in love to my child, who briefly needed Mom again.

I face an empty nest without the comfort of a mate to share the pain and joy. I journey alone without an older generation to cushion the unknown future and with a painful suspicion that the genes I inherited may in fact carry me into a long life, but not necessarily a healthy one. Which do I prefer: an inventive, inquiring mind or a body that, like the Duracell bunny, keeps on going, minus the memories? Old age does not look particularly inviting right now.

And just in case these losses are not enough, I now face the prospect of having to leave my home of more than thirty years. The city this country girl made her own so many years ago has become too expensive for me to live in. I will have to leave our apartment, which Pros so carefully chose for us; leave our Church family, which has embraced and nurtured us; leave the neighborhood where my daughters played and grew and went to school. This begins to feel like more than I can bear.

When my husband died, I hurled questions into that great, dark void where even in my pain and anger I trusted God still reigned and cared. "Why me, God?" and "Why my husband?" were only the first. Soon, I stumbled from stunned disbelief into "How?" and "How will I survive?" In our world of couples, how would I shed the garments of widowhood and move in the world as just Jane, and not "Prosper and Jane"?

Now it feels as if there are no more garments to shed. My anger long ago spent, I stand alone, numb and frozen, unable to move. Fearfully I whisper: "What do I do now, God? Where do I go?" And God is strangely silent.

In my long journey as widow and single parent, I have cherished the counsel of the poet Rainer Maria Rilke. I have honored the questions, trying to be patient with all that is unsolved in my heart, not seeking answers, "which cannot be given you because you would not be able to live them. And the point is, to live everything. *Live* the questions now. Perhaps you will then gradually, without noticing it, live along some distant day into the answer."[1]

This bleak landscape of loss and pain is familiar. I traveled here sixteen years ago, seventeen summers ago, when Prosper died. My body still remembers what it feels like to slam against that cold stone wall of Death and in pain and despair shake my fist and scream, "Why?" My heart still holds the memory of walking, stumbling mostly, hand in hand with God. I have learned that it is not in our seeking the answer to "Why?" but in living out the "How?" that God works out the abundance of life God has promised us.

With so many sad endings, I have arrived at another beginning. Where shall I go from here, leaving behind my life as a widow and the daily cares and joys of parenting? I can live on into an uncertain future carrying my mother's and father's memories in my heart. I can stand alone on that shifting ground between this world and the next, serving as a protective guardian of my own children's hopes and dreams. *But how do I leave my home?*

I move in the spaciousness of this life I have been blessed with, just Jane now, still living the questions. I can only trust that God will lead me into the "how."

Anne

As the first anniversary of David's death approached, I was apprehensive. It had been a painful year of "firsts" without him—first holidays, birthdays, wedding anniversary. I had also been struggling with memories of the events of the year before: "Last year at this time he started having back pain . . . was taken to the hospital . . . began chemotherapy . . ." Those memories were so upsetting that I worried about how I might feel when the death anniversary arrived. At the same time, there continued to be a number of difficult practical details to take care of.

Several years ago, after a close friend of ours died, David had investigated whether he and I could have two of the unoccupied plots in the section of the Jewish cemetery where many of his relatives were buried. He found out that he could be buried there, but I, as a non-Jew, could not be. So he told me he wished to be buried with me somewhere else and suggested that we go cemetery shopping. I replied that I didn't want to do that yet, because I was sure he had many years left to live. Besides, I went on, I expected our lack of "burial property" to serve as an extra incentive for both of us to avoid any need to be buried. We joked about that for a few minutes and then dropped the subject.

On the November night in the hospital when his doctors first thought he was about to die, however, I realized I could no longer hide from the question of cemetery plots. And now I was going to have to go looking for them without David's help.

The next morning I drove to the only nonsectarian cemetery I knew of in Brooklyn—beautiful, historic Green-Wood—a short distance from where David was born. I stumbled numbly alongside the "memorial counselor" across a small hill with plots available where a path used to be. I chose a spot for David and me and paid for it with my credit card. I listened mutely as the salesman went over all the procedures and regulations and told me what to do in the event that burial became necessary during the upcoming Thanksgiving weekend.

Back at home after his month in the hospital, David and I exchanged stories about our experiences during that terrifying time. My stories included the gravesite purchase. Despite the now-perceptible approach of his death, he laughed for the first time in weeks when I described how the two of us would be housed for eternity as neighbors of Samuel Morse, an inventor he admired, and the Brooks Brothers, his favorite clothiers.

By summer David had been laid to rest in Green-Wood, and the time had come to make arrangements for a monument. Even though he wasn't buried with his forebears, I wanted the gravestone to reflect theirs in some way. So I paid a visit to their cemetery in Long Island. Several of the older stones in the family plot were so covered with ivy that it was difficult to find them. Standing alone under the August sun, tears flowing down my face, I told his parents and grandparents how grateful I was to have had such a wonderful man to love. Surrounded as far as the eye could see by acres of silent granite, I explained to them why he wasn't buried with them. I thanked my mother-in-law for the graciousness with which she, a Jewish widow like the biblical Naomi, had received me as a prospective daughter-in-law. I carefully copied the spelling of the Hebrew names. The next day I returned with my gardening tools and freed the stones from the overgrown ivy.

Ours would be a shared headstone. After deliberating for months, what I finally chose as the first words on it were from Psalm 23: "I will fear no evil for Thou art with me." I thought this verse would be fitting for both of us for several reasons. When David walked courageously through the valley of the shadow of death, I'd ultimately had to turn him over to the care of God. I hoped to be united with him and God when I walked through the valley myself someday, and until then I longed for their presence in my earthly life. And finally, David was in that cemetery because of his wish to be buried with me. The Psalm verse would be followed by his Hebrew name, *David ben Shalom Moshe*; his English name; and his dates of birth and death; with room underneath for the eventual addition of my name and dates.

The next task was to find a monument company that was Jewish enough to get the Hebrew lettering right but not Jewish enough to make me feel bad about how I'd married him or buried him. "Authorized Jewish and Nonsectarian for All Cemeteries," declared a Yellow Pages ad for one establishment; "Inscriptions in Any Language." That sounded about right.

At the monument office, I was strangely composed as I discussed wording, lettering, material, design, and price with the manager. In fact, there was something about the task that was unexpectedly comforting. "I ordered our monument on Tuesday," I wrote in one of my letters to David a few days later. "The headstone is for both of us, and I will fear no evil because you and God are with me. We will be together there."

The stone was set in place the following spring. It was just as I'd ordered—light gray granite, unpolished except for a simple border, with the lettering I'd specified. I had been looking forward to seeing the finished memorial. But the first time I saw it, the main feeling I had was discomfort—embarrassment, almost.

Traditionally, Jews are supposed to marry Jews and be buried in Jewish cemeteries. I cringed as I looked around and imagined how David's Orthodox older relatives would react to his being in this place, not far from monuments adorned with crucifixes or Russian icons or pictures of Jesus and Mary with thorn-circled hearts. I tried to remind myself that being buried in Green-Wood was my husband's wish. He had been so centered, so sure of himself, that he was practically never troubled by what people might think. I began to search within myself for that kind of confidence. But then more issues cropped up.

"I hope your kids aren't bothered by the 'Thou art with me' Bible verse, which is a lot about us, instead of something like 'Husband, Father, Grandfather' like so many other monuments have," I wrote in another letter to David as soon as I got home. "Some of the people coming to the unveiling are atheists. I didn't even consult anyone else about the stone. In normal families they probably do this together. What was I *thinking*? Have I done something wrong? Why don't you come back here and help me deal with this?"

It is a Jewish custom to unveil and dedicate a grave marker around the first anniversary of a death. Someone once told me that the name for the ceremony may date back to an era when gravestones were sent to the cemetery wrapped in burlap to keep them from being damaged in the horse-drawn vehicles that transported them; "unveiling" meant taking the fabric cover off a stone once it was in place. Family and close friends gather at the gravesite, recite prayers and psalms, remove a covering (usually cheesecloth nowadays) from the monument, and speak about the deceased.

David's children and I decided to have an unveiling ceremony on the exact anniversary of his death. With their spouses and David's brother's widow, they came from far and near to the cemetery. The late-April day was unseasonably warm and sunny, just as it had been a year before when we watched his casket being lowered into ground now covered with grass. Psalm 23 was among the Scripture passages we read, as well as Ecclesiastes 3:1–8 and portions of Psalm 90. We recited the Mourner's Kaddish[2] and *El Malei Rachamim* ("God, Full of Compassion . . .").[3] People commented that the monument was elegant and tasteful. No one seemed bothered by the fact that it butted up against another grave marker that had a rosary and a cross inscribed on it. As we left, each of us placed on the grave a small stone brought from home. Then we spent the afternoon sharing memories in the favorite restaurant where we had enjoyed many a meal when David was with us.

There were ten of us that day: seven plus three, the numbers that signify completeness.

In the company of the family who had become my family, I found this deliberate and formal observance of the anniversary enormously healing. The occasion turned out so well, I could hardly remember why I'd been uncomfortable not long before. Maybe it wasn't really about lines from Scripture or the type of cemetery in which David was buried. Maybe it was about the fact that when he died he was married to me, not to either of the mothers of his children. Maybe it was about the ultimate intimacy of his desire to lie there with me, his bones mingled with mine in the sandy soil of Brooklyn, for all time. In a plot I'd picked out myself, near two enormous copper beech trees that had been planted on opposite sides of the road but had grown together at the top. And my attempts to respond to that desire in words carved into a monument of solid granite, boldly set out for all to see.

As I read aloud at the unveiling, "For love is strong as death, passion fierce as the grave. . . . If one offered for love all the wealth of one's house, it would be utterly scorned" (Song of Solomon 8:6–7).

chapter six

❊

Anna

Luke 2:36–38

HER HUSBAND DIED AFTER THEY HAD been married only seven years, leaving her a young widow. Now she is elderly, eighty-four years old. She has been a widow for more than half a century, having never remarried. She does not have children to protect or who can offer her companionship and provision. Alone, she spends every moment at the Jerusalem Temple, worshiping "there with fasting and prayer night and day" (Luke 2:37).

Why is she there? What does she seek? What is it about the life and worship of the Temple that sustain her?

On a practical level, we might understand Anna's proximity to the Temple as her only means for daily survival. Because she has no husband or child, and because she is elderly, she is among the most economically vulnerable of her society. She is no longer physically able to glean the agricultural fields for leftover grains and fruits, as poor widows were legally permitted to do in order not to starve. Her life may depend on alms she might receive from pilgrims visiting the Temple.

Anna's story, however, is not manifestly about a widow's economic destitution and helplessness. In this, her story differs from many about widows in the Bible, including elsewhere in Luke's Gospel.[1] We have no sense that Anna is impoverished, anxious, or desperate.[2] She does not beg, demand justice, or seek a new husband for security. Rather, she prays without ceasing. She seems to be yearning for something that is not practical at all.

Part of the narrative of Jesus' birth in Luke's Gospel, Anna's story comes immediately after the story of Simeon (see Luke 2:25–35), an older man to whom the Holy Spirit had revealed that he would see the Messiah before his death. Often in Luke's Gospel, two stories are paired, one whose main character is male, the other female, for literary emphasis. Such is the pairing of Simeon and Anna. Both are elderly. Simeon is "righteous and devout" (2:25), while Anna worships continually in the Temple. Anna's name means "favor" or "grace." The Holy Spirit "rested on" Simeon (2:25), a characteristic of the Hebrew prophets, and Anna, herself, is called a "prophet" (2:36). According to Luke's Gospel, both Simeon and Anna behold the Messiah when Mary and Joseph bring the baby Jesus to the Temple.[3]

Simeon, therefore, may offer us a hint about what Anna is seeking. At a time when the Jewish people are under the rule of a foreign power, the Roman Empire, Simeon "is looking forward to the consolation of Israel" (Luke 2:25) by the coming of the Messiah, who will break the bonds of oppression and lead the people into freedom. In her prayer Anna also might be yearning for Israel's deliverance. Her prayer does include fasting, a common biblical act of devotion, contrition, and an appeal to God by the Jewish people in times of national distress. On seeing Jesus she begins to praise God, as Simeon did,[4] and also "to speak about the child to all who were looking for the redemption of Jerusalem" (2:38).

We wonder, though, if her prayer might also have a personal dimension. Simeon seeks the consolation of Israel, but he does not, like Anna, pray unceasingly in the Temple. Nor is he a widow.

For biblical people, fasting was also an expression of personal grief. When King David learned of the death of Saul, for example, he tore his clothes and fasted in mourning (see 2 Samuel 1:11–12). Among Anna's biblical forebears, most similar to her is the mother of Samuel, Hannah, who, in the Hebrew language, shares Anna's name. Before she gave birth to the prophet, despairing that she was elderly and childless, Hannah "wept and would not eat" (1 Samuel 1:7). Her husband, Elkanah, worried, "Hannah, why do you weep? Why do you not eat? Why is your heart sad? Am I not more to you than ten sons?" (1:8). Like Anna, Hannah also went to a place of worship to pray fervently. She presented herself at the house of the Lord in Shiloh, the central sanctuary of the Israelites in her day, and confessed to the priest Eli, "I am a woman deeply troubled" (1:15). Hannah's prayer in the Shiloh temple was specifically for a male child: "O Lord of hosts, if only you will look on the misery of your servant, and remember me, and not forget your servant, but will give to your servant a male child, then I will set him before you as a nazirite[5] until the day of his death" (1:11). God granted her petition through the birth of Samuel.

Anna's prayer with fasting might be, therefore, like Hannah's, an expression of grief over being elderly and childless. Perhaps Anna also is longing for a child.

Still, Anna is a widow, not a wife like Hannah. Nor does she seem to be seeking a husband. The years of her marriage, *seven*, a number in the Jewish tradition signifying wholeness and completion, suggest that her marriage ended as it should, within a time appointed by God. She does not seem to be seeking a child *of her own*. Furthermore, Anna is continually at the Jerusalem Temple praying, whereas Hannah visited the sanctuary in Shiloh only during the annual pilgrimage. Does the Jerusalem Temple have special significance for Anna's prayer, revealing a yet more profound yearning?

According to the faith of the Jewish people, the Jerusalem Temple was the house of God, the place where God chose to dwell. Pilgrims journeyed from faraway to the Temple to sing the Psalms, offer sacrifices to God, and fulfill their vows to the Most High. They came also, perhaps especially, to draw near to God, as close as they could imagine.

Is this Anna's deepest longing? To be as near to God as possible? Is that why she prays in the Temple day and night? During his public ministry, Jesus will fast in prayer in order to draw close to God, to empty himself of his own desires, to abide more fully in God's love. By her prayer and fasting, is Anna similarly seeking a closer relationship with God?

If so, the story of Anna is especially moving because she is a woman. In the Jerusalem Temple, she must worship in the Court of the Women. The Temple includes several courts, each drawing closer to the Holy of Holies, the innermost chamber, in the darkness of which God resides. The outermost court of the Temple is the Court of the Gentiles, then comes the Court of the Women. Beyond this place where Anna worships is the Court of Israel, into which only Jewish men can enter, and finally, closest to the Holy of Holies, is the Court of Priests. Desiring to approach God, Anna must remain farther away, at least physically, from the presence of God than the men of her faith community.

In all, Anna's prayer is complex and layered. Like Simeon, she seems to pray for the deliverance of the Jewish people. Like Hannah, she seems to pray for a child. Within the deepest place of her heart, she seems to pray that she might draw nearer to God. Perhaps in her unceasing prayer, she prays most fervently the Psalms that express this last, most profound desire: "As a deer longs for flowing streams, / so my soul longs for you, O God" (42:1).

> One thing I asked of the LORD,
>   that I will seek after:
> to live in the house of the LORD
>   all the days of my life,
> to behold the beauty of the LORD,
>   and to inquire in his temple.
> (27:4)

When Anna beholds the baby Jesus in the Temple, God graciously answers her prayer in all its texture and nuance. If she has prayed for the deliverance of Israel, like Simeon she now sees, according to Christian belief, the Messiah who will offer redemption. If she has prayed for a child, now a child is before her eyes. The baby Jesus, born to Mary, is a gift for all people, including Anna.[6] If she has prayed to draw closer to God, she now is nearer to the presence of God, in Jesus, than ever before. God is no longer hidden just beyond her reach. God is intimately close. God can be held in her arms.

Perhaps it is this very personal experience of God, in answer to her prayer, that inspires Anna to become one of the earliest evangelists. In the very moment she encounters Jesus in the Temple, she begins "to speak about the child to all" (Luke 2:38).

Why is it that we go to church? For the comfort of ritual prayer? To be with other people, especially when we feel alone? To find support, even economic help, in times of need? These are certainly reasons why Anna may have worshiped at the Jerusalem Temple.

Or is it that we, like Anna, yearn in the deepest part of ourselves to draw nearer to God? Do we seek a personal encounter with the holy? Do we dare to believe that Jesus might offer us this gift? Will we, like Anna, find Jesus in the sanctuary? And wherever we find Jesus, and however we come to behold the something we long for, yet so surprising, fresh, and lovely in its manifestation, won't we wish to tell everyone?

❀

Prayer and Meditation

For Widows
- How have you felt about God since the death of your loved one?
- Did the death raise any theological questions for you?
- Did you attend religious services after the death? Do you now?
- How has your prayer changed?

For All
- What is it like for you to grow older?
- How long have you belonged to your particular faith community? Are you growing in intimacy there with others? With God?
- In times of personal difficulty, do you tend to withdraw from your community of faith, in anger or embarrass-

ment, or do you turn to them, with honesty, for consolation and encouragement?

• Remember a moment when you felt great hope because
of a very small thing.

• Away from church, meditate on Psalm 27:4. Then, do
so in church. Do you notice a difference?

◎〜◎

Anne

People who are grieving often wrestle with big, painful
theological questions, along these lines:

"Oh, Lord, *why* did she have to die?"

"Why didn't Jesus answer our prayers and make him get
well?"

"What kind of a God would allow an innocent child to
suffer like that?"

"What the hell does it mean when people say this was 'part
of God's plan for her'?"

"Did he die because God was punishing him? or me?"

"Why did this have to happen now? in my life? the way it
did?"

For me, the question that occupied much of my attention
after David's death was, *Where is he now?*

Life had departed from his body while I watched. The
monitor at his bedside showed heartbeats until the moment
when it abruptly stopped showing them. Then it registered a
few more sporadic pulses, as if a question had arisen about
whether it was time for him to go yet after all. Then the line
went flat again, and stayed flat. The appearance of his face
changed in a subtle way that I can't describe and that
reflected, somehow, the sudden lack of his presence. A young
resident came in, listened intently with a stethoscope, and
told us there were no longer any vital signs. Recalling
accounts I'd read of near-death experiences in which "clini-
cally dead" people hovered near the ceiling looking down at
their bodies and the people in the room, I looked up often for
the next few minutes to see if I could see some sign of David
there. I couldn't.

He was gone. But where did he go? Does he still exist in some form? If he is somewhere else now, is he happy there? Will I ever see him again? Can he see me now? Does he miss me? If I write a letter to him today, will he know what it says?

Despite the apparent urgency of the questions people ask, the period of bereavement might not be the ideal time for serious theological discussions about death. Even if someone were able to provide me with God's absolute truth about why David died, would that ease my grief? Indeed, if *God* were to appear to me and explain why all the prayers offered for David's recovery from illness seem not to have had the desired effect, would that make me miss him any less? Could it be that all the *whys* and *whats* that we cry out really mean something like "I am hurt/frightened/angry! Say something to make it better!"?

Many of us who have lost a loved one feel angry at God and/or the person who died. In the months after David's death, I usually preferred to get angry at people who said things I didn't like about the afterlife.

Where was David? Depending on the theological proclivities of the person offering the opinion, he was:

- nowhere
- somewhere, awaiting the Messiah and final bodily resurrection
- in heaven, in the presence of God and maybe his ancestors
- in purgatory for a while, atoning for the sins of his earthly life
- in hell for eternity, having not been baptized or accepted Jesus as his personal savior during his earthly life
- "on the other side," not far away and perhaps accessible for contact with us
- reincarnated, or preparing for reincarnation, in another body for another lifetime
- absorbed into God

The thought of David's being in some of those places made me uncomfortable, and some were places where I heartily hoped he would never be. Also, a number of people described to me their experiences of seeing or hearing from their deceased loved ones; a few even said they carried on conversations with them. But I was not having any such experiences. What, I wondered, did that mean?

The more discussions I had about David's whereabouts, the more upset I got. I couldn't help thinking of the theological formulations Job's friends offered to account for Job's miserable circumstances. Why can't we just admit that we really don't know what happens to people after they die, I began to wonder? Whatever the truth is about the afterlife, it is probably no more comprehensible to our limited human minds than is the idea of God.

"I hate religion!" I finally burst out in exasperation to my friend Janey, after recounting to her yet another after-death theory that disturbed me. "Theology is *hubris*!" Then, after a pause, I started to laugh. Really, I didn't have to take to heart everything I heard on that subject—especially after Janey had T-shirts made for both of us with "Theology is hubris" printed in big red and black letters. It was a relief to be able to laugh off some of the pain of wondering what had become of David.

The biblical Anna, prophet and holy woman, seems to have lived into an extraordinarily close connection with God during her many decades of widowhood. Had she ever wondered what became of her husband after he died? Did her constant presence in the Temple signify that she had found an answer to that question that satisfied her—or was she perhaps still looking for one?

At this much earlier stage of loss, my experience of God has fluctuated widely. Throughout the illness that led up to David's death, I had to call on God for help in making it through, four hours at a time. I also begged God to make my husband well again. Even though I knew (intellectually, at least) that no one is exempt from the suffering and death that are inevitable parts of the human condition, I was sometimes angry. When other patients in the chemotherapy center moved toward the cures or remissions that were not in store for David, I couldn't help wondering whether they might be more valued and cherished by God than we were. Some people were getting well, so why wasn't he? During one particularly anguished episode, I described God as "a negligent, uncaring, unhelpful, largely absent entity that I would like to kick in the teeth, stab with a knife, shove over a cliff, and blow up with a nuclear warhead." Fortunately, as Lisa Belcher Hamilton, author of *For Those We Love But See No Longer*, put it, "I've learned that times when my anger might be judged blasphemous seem to be used particularly well by God to deepen our relationship."[7]

Since David's death, I have been surprised by changes in how I think of and imagine God. Nowadays I am often drawn to lean on the powerful deity of Psalm 46, the God who stands up to rage and tumult, wrestles with Jacob, and breaks, shatters, and burns up our human-made weapons. And I am especially attracted to the person of Jesus—the strong, welcoming carpenter who befriended women and outcasts; the Jewish man who voiced unpopular truths and faced an agonizing death with courage. I have appreciated feminine and gender-neutral God imagery in the past, but I do not find such imagery very attractive right now. I like men and miss my husband intensely; the God I reach out to now is decidedly masculine—and reminds me a bit of David.

Is God omnipotent? Does God intervene in our lives? Does God suffer when we suffer? Does God care about us at all? I know there is a difference between being "cured" and being "healed," and I know that a response to prayer does not necessarily comply with the request made. I don't know why illness exists. I don't know why David got an incurable form of cancer. I don't know that it was "part of God's plan" for him, nor do I wish to believe it was designed as a punishment. One thing I do know is that I am grateful for the time we had together before he died. I am grateful that he found the courage to hold on to life as passionately as he did. I am grateful that he died with the people he loved around him. These were certainly not the answers to prayer that I was hoping for, but perhaps they were answers nonetheless.

"Take care of him. Take care of me." Since David died, these have been the last words I utter to God before going to sleep every night. If he has survived death in some way, then what I care about most is that he be safe and well, wherever he is. Barbara Cawthorne Crafton once wrote about some people who used to come to her healing services years ago and were now dead. "All healed now, perfect and joyful and alive," she said of them.[8] And in a condolence message, my friend Carol, a Lutheran pastor, spoke of my surrendering David into the loving hands of God. "You know that he is not lost to you forever," she continued, "but has only preceded you into that home for which we all long and hope." Ah, yes. Whatever these statements may mean, they put into words my fondest wish for my cherished husband.

Jane

One evening recently, when I was in a blue funk deep enough to wallow in, I wailed, "I have no friends!" Radiating concern, her brow furrowed, Whitney admonished: "Mom, you can't just assume someone is a friend. You have to *be* with her. You have to *call* her, *talk* to her, *hang out* with her. Being a friend takes work, Mom!" Now, I admit that I, a confirmed introvert who nine times out of ten prefers the company of a good book, can be accused of neglecting my friends.

There are, however, three relationships that I have worked to nurture over the years. The first two are with each of my daughters. Parenting has been a deeply satisfying and rewarding experience. Having weathered birth pains, helpless infancy, toddlers into everything, best-buddy-I-will-never-leave-you grade school years, and smart-aleck-impossible-to-live-with preteens, I am now almost on the other side of adolescence. (Think terrible twos with tattoos; belly rings; almost bare, thin curvy bodies; and minds that leap ahead with arguments that would sway a Supreme Court justice before you can open your mouth to say "no.") I have discovered the rich rewards of being "Mom" to beautiful young women.

The third relationship that calls me out of myself is with God.

God and I have talked for as long as I have memory. My happiest early memories are of church. As a child, God was defined by the parameters of a simple wood-framed building, warm bodies, swishing paper fans advertising a local funeral home, a mother quieting a fussy child at her breast, lusty hymn singing, and interminable sermons rising to a crescendo that signaled a welcome end and time for games outside with the other children. During my adolescence the relationship became more fraught with tension and expectation. I felt called by God but unable to discern or articulate what was happening within my heart and soul. In my small Bible-Belt farming community, women and girls were not encouraged to explore much beyond marriage and raising children, and I was without a spiritual guide.

Eventually, I went away to college and discovered boys. God was put on hold for many years while I met and married Prosper and moved to New York City. It wasn't until I became a mother myself that my need for a closer walk with God reasserted itself.

The two years prior to Pros's death became a time of heady spiritual growth for me. As I finally found the support I needed to explore my sense of call, my relationship with God was nurtured and matured. My marriage was stabilizing; I was learning to keep the focus on myself and leave Pros's new-found sobriety to himself. Our daughters were a source of joy and pleasure, and we delighted in them. We attended Grace Church regularly as a family. I taught Sunday school and participated in both a lay preaching group and a Bible study group. I became a familiar fixture at Grace, often hauling baby Whitney, secure in her Snuggli, along with me. I recall cold winter evenings as the wind rattled the windows of the room where we were gathered for study; my fussy baby was passed from one willing seeker to another as we read and pondered the Bible.

When the long hot days of summer rolled around, my friend Nancy and I planned a week of Vacation Bible School. In the small rural town where I grew up, Vacation Bible

School had been standard. As a teen I was a co-teacher under my mother's firm guidance. Why not try it at Grace Church? Eight children (including our own four) of various ages signed up; Whitney, in her little bouncing seat, was the youngest. During a week of steamy August heat, the children took turns entertaining Whitney while we built a papier-mâché mountain, shared Bible stories of meeting God on the mountain, and visited the Cloisters museum in the upper reaches of Manhattan. As we nurtured and led our small flock, I met God time and again on mountains of delight. God was calling, and I eagerly leaped to answer. Life felt rich with promise and blessing.

Then, into this growing relationship, this good abundance, God dropped a bomb and blew my world, as I knew it, apart.

Although God and I met nightly in the weeks and months that became the first year after Pros's death, from the time the girls went to bed until sometimes 3:00 a.m., I would not have termed it a "friendly" relationship. From my point of view, our relationship had suffered a serious breakdown. Hadn't I kept my end of what I thought, in my naiveté, were the terms of our relationship? I was exploring God's call, leading the way for my family and others. Following a good Christian life. Doing all and more of what I felt I ought to. Doing it not out of a sense of obligation, but with joy and childlike delight in all the pleasures to be found in loving God. God had betrayed me, and I wanted a divorce.

Yet, God continued to be my constant companion.

In those nightly encounters, I, like Job, shook my fist and ranted and raved. Like Abraham, I bargained and obeyed. Like Sarah, I laughed in derision. And I felt God's presence hovering, sometimes almost palpable.

My journal was filled with my anger, fear, and deep sense of betrayal. But it was my dreams that offered me hope.

My dreams were often of journeys, myself and my daughters traveling somewhere, and always there hovered a mysterious shadowy figure, usually male, who was our guide or pilot or driver. In one of the first of those dreams, I heard the driver say, as he pulled away after dropping us off at some unknown destination, "I would move heaven and earth to be with you, if only I could." I wanted to assume that, in every dream, the shadowy figure was Pros, still loving me, still watching out for us from the other side of Death. I do believe that to be true. But I also understand that the Guide was God. Either way, I would wake, sobbing my heartbreak, but strangely comforted. Gradually my writing changed. Powered by the same passion that drove the anger, and soaring above the hurt and pain, were my love songs to God.

In February 1989, at the beginning of Lent, about nine months after Pros's death, I wrote:

> I have begun another descent. The peak was high this time—the air rare and holy. I thought at times that I surely would burst. Now I feel weary and bereft again. But with a difference. There is within me a new sense of strength that is mine and yet not mine, a Power, a sureness. I don't know where I am going, but I know that God leads me. And I carry God's love within me. It burns bright and steady, sometimes flaring up and lighting the world around me, giving an intensity and urgency to life. Sometimes it burns quietly, but always there. . . . How can anyone not choose to love God?

It has been sixteen years and four months since my husband died. Like my biblical sister, Anna, I have remained in my church, worshiping, praying, and serving. Over the years I settled into a comfortable routine, teaching Sunday school, attending prayer group and Bible study, and serving as a member of the vestry and chairperson of the Christian Formation Committee.

I feel comfortable and secure in God's love, but lately have found myself growing weary of the service and longing for the intensity of those months after Pros died, when God was so close and I was so passionate. Once again I feel God's call to come deeper, and my soul leaps within me. I am gradually disentangling myself from many of my parish activities. I am taking a year off, a year of prayer and contemplation, a year of writing and talking with God. Like Anna, with only Grace Church's courtyard separating me from the sanctuary, I will worship, pray, and give thanks to God for this good abundance of life.

chapter seven

❈

Judith

Judith 8:1–16:25

SHE COMES INTO HER OWN, as a faithful Jew who prays to God, as a woman who is beautiful and sexual, and as a heroine who rescues the Israelites from defeat by a seemingly invincible foreign nation. It takes years after the death of her husband for her beauty and power to reemerge, but when they do, she wins victory for her people and so their hearts.

Sexuality is present in the stories of several biblical widows, but most strikingly in the Book of Judith.[1] Usually the sexuality of biblical widows appears only within the context of the traditional biblical roles for women of wife and mother. Tamar tricks Judah into sleeping with her, for example, in order to become pregnant and thereby ensure her economic security and the ongoing lineage of the patriarchs. Ruth similarly uses her sexuality to invite Boaz into a marriage that will protect her and her mother-in-law, Naomi, also a widow, against impoverishment. Like Tamar, Ruth will bear a son whose descendants will include King David and Jesus. For these widows, the moment in which they draw upon their sexuality is ambiguous in detail and carries an aura of social shame. Both the purpose of their sexual acts and the "lowered eyes" character of the storytelling serve to temper, for us, the force of the widows' sexuality. By contrast, we discover Judith to be a beautiful woman who boldly uses her sexual appeal in a protracted seduction of an enemy general in order to become not a wife and mother but rather a triumphant warrior.

The setting for Judith's story is the rise to world power of the Assyrians, ruled by King Nebuchadnezzar and led militarily by the fierce general Holofernes. (Immediately we recognize the Book of Judith as a work of literature rather than world history, because Nebuchadnezzar actually ruled in Babylon, not Assyria.) The Israelites have returned to Judea after a long exile and are now watching Nebuchadnezzar and Holofernes engage in a military campaign to conquer the nations of the biblical world. One by one all the nations either are destroyed or become vassal states. Judea is suddenly left alone to face the bruising power and ambition of the Assyrians. In an appeal to God, the Israelites begin to fast, put on sackcloth and ashes, and pray for deliverance. They also start to fortify the Judean hilltops and the mountain passes into Judea and to stockpile food in preparation for war.

Holofernes is determined to wage war, and soon blocks the supply of water into the town of Bethulia, where the war begins. The crisis becomes acute. For thirty-four days the Assyrians surround the town. The water containers and cisterns run dry, and the Israelites begin to collapse in the street from thirst. Under pressure from the people, Uzziah, a leader of the Israelites, pledges to give God only five more days to show mercy and bring about deliverance. After the five days, he and the other Israelite leaders will surrender to the Assyrians in order to end the people's misery.

Into this dire situation, unexpectedly, the widow Judith steps forward. For more than three years since the death of her husband, Manasseh, she has lived quietly and prayerfully as a widow in a tent on the roof of her house,[2] wearing sackcloth around her waist, dressing in widow's garments and fasting in mourning. But the news of Uzziah's oath to surrender the town causes her to summon the leaders. She is stunned by their arrogance before God and argues with theological conviction that they have erred by testing God. "No, my brothers, do not anger the Lord our God. For if he does not choose to help us within these five days, he has the power to protect us within any time he pleases, or even to destroy us in the presence of our enemies. Do not try to bind the purposes of the Lord our God; for God is not like a human being, to be threatened, or like a mere mortal, to be won over by pleading. Therefore, while we wait for his deliverance, let us call upon him to help us, and he will hear our voice, if it pleases him" (Judith 8:14–17). For Judith, prayer should not seek to force God into providing a favorable outcome; rather, it must involve submission to God's purposes. All of Judea, including the Temple in Jerusalem, she adds, is depending on the ability of Bethulia to withstand the Assyrians. "In spite of everything let us give thanks to the Lord our God," she urges (8:25). Uzziah acknowledges her wisdom yet maintains that he has made an oath he cannot break. "Now since you are a God-fearing woman, pray for us," he implores, "so that the Lord may send us rain to fill our cisterns" (8:31).

Her theological argument set aside, Judith resolves to take dramatic action. "Listen to me. I am about to do something that will go down through all generations of our descendants" (Judith 8:32). She will not reveal her plan but simply asks Uzziah to offer her and her maid protection that night so that they may depart from the town in safety. He agrees.

Once the leaders depart, Judith prostrates herself, puts ashes on her head, and offers a lengthy prayer to God. She asks for neither God's intervention nor guidance. She asks, instead, for strength. Combining prayer with bold initiative, she is resolved. Her prayer opens with intimations of sexuality. "O Lord God of my ancestor Simeon, to whom you gave a sword to take revenge on those strangers who had torn off a virgin's clothing to defile her, and exposed her thighs to put her to shame, and polluted her womb to disgrace her. . . . O God, my God, hear me also, a widow" (Judith 9:2,4). Acknowledging that any success in her endeavor will be God's alone, she prays, "Give to me, a widow, the strong hand to do what I plan. . . . Let your whole nation and every tribe know and understand that you are God, the God of all power and might, and that there is no other who protects the people of Israel but you alone!" (9:9,14).

After her prayer, Judith rises and, for the first time in years, begins to adorn herself in order to be sexually attractive. The scene plays slowly, and we notice every detail. She removes the sackcloth she had been wearing and the widow's garments. She bathes her body and anoints herself with precious ointment. She combs her hair, puts on a tiara, and dresses in the festive garments she used to wear when her husband was still living. She puts on anklets, bracelets, rings, earrings. A beautiful woman, she now endeavors to become also enticing.

We might feel prurient as we watch Judith's preparations were we not aware of the moment's emotional poignancy. In her prayer Judith had revealed how much she still views herself as a widow. After Manasseh's death she had grieved far longer than customary. Although Jewish law did not command specific mourning periods, rabbinic oral interpretation of the law, later to be codified in the Talmud, encouraged people not to mourn excessively. Grieving was most intense in the days immediately following the death, including the seven-day period of *shivah*, during which mourners received condolences from the community. Thereafter people might continue to observe mourning customs—dressing in sackcloth, fasting, abstaining from anointing oil and ornamentation, and not attending festive gatherings—yet the mourning would usually end sometime within the first year after the loved one's death. Judith has grieved for three years and four months. Now, as she adorns herself, she must let go of the familiar mourning customs. She must open herself to the future, including again being sexually attractive.

When Judith emerges in public, heads turn. At the town gate, Uzziah and the elders are stunned by her transformation and "very greatly astounded at her beauty" (Judith 10:7). So are the men of the Assyrian patrol, who soon capture Judith and her maid. Judith convinces the enemy patrol that she is seeking refuge because the Assyrians, under Holofernes' command, will surely be victorious over the Israelites. She tells them she will spy for them. So they take her to Holofernes' tent. As she enters the Assyrian camp, the people mistakenly assume that all Israelites are as lovely as Judith, not realizing that the Israelites, ironically, are presently dressed in the very sackcloth and ashes Judith has taken off. "Who can despise these people, who have women like this among them?" they ask. "It is not wise to leave one of their men alive, for if we let them go they will be able to beguile the whole world!" (10:19).

Judith's intent is to beguile only Holofernes. His guards lead her into the general's tent, and as she comes into his presence, his servants marvel at the beauty of her face. Holofernes tells her not to fear and asks her why she has come. Judith then tells him an elaborate lie. Nebuchadnezzar is king of the whole earth, she flatters him, but the people serve the king only because of the general's power. Flirtatiously, she tells Holofernes that he alone is "the best in the whole kingdom, the most informed and the most astounding in military strength" (Judith 11:8). Because the food supply in Bethulia is almost exhausted, she adds, the Israelites are about to sin by eating foods consecrated to God. This will anger God, who will hand them over to Holofernes. "God has sent me," Judith woos, "to accomplish with you things that will astonish the whole world wherever people shall hear about them" (11:16). All Holofernes has to do is wait, allowing Judith to go out of the Assyrian camp each night and into the valley to pray. God will tell her when the Israelites have sinned, and Holofernes will gain victory over Bethulia and all Judea.

Judith's words please Holofernes, who agrees to her plan. His servants are astounded. "No other woman from one end of the earth to the other looks so beautiful or speaks so wisely!" (Judith 11:21).

Judith then begins her slow, teasing seduction. For three days she lives in Holofernes' tent. She is faithful in observing Jewish law by not eating with Holofernes, a Gentile, and by bathing in the valley for purification before prayer. Yet she also artfully does so under the general's eye, making sure he knows when she is going out to bathe. It is a scene reminiscent of King David watching the lovely Bathsheba bathe. Holofernes' desire builds.[3] On the fourth day, he tells his eunuch, "Go and persuade the Hebrew woman who is in your care to join us and to eat and drink with us. For it would be a disgrace if we let such a woman go without having intercourse with her. If we do not seduce her, she will laugh at us" (Judith 12:11–12).

The eunuch extends the general's invitation for Judith to join him at a banquet. "Whatever pleases him I will do at once," Judith hints (Judith 12:14). She then dresses in all her finery and, just before Holofernes arrives at the banquet, lies down on some lambskins on the ground.

When Holofernes beholds Judith, his heart is "ravished with her and his passion [is] aroused" (Judith 12:16). Giddily, he invites her to drink wine with him. "I will gladly drink, my lord, because today is the greatest day in my whole life" (12:18). Quite pleased, Holofernes begins to drink more wine, "much more than he had ever drunk in any one day since he was born" (12:20). Soon he passes out on his bed.

When evening comes, Holofernes' servants and Judith's maid withdraw, leaving the general and Judith alone. Judith stands beside the bed and prays in her heart for God to glorify Jerusalem by her design and to give her strength. Taking his own sword, she strikes Holofernes' neck twice with all her might and cuts off his head. She rolls his body off the bed and steals the bed's canopy. Then, she goes out to her waiting maid, who puts Holofernes' head into their food bag. Together they escape into the night, seemingly going out as they have every previous night to pray.

When they reach the gates of Bethulia, Uzziah and the people run to greet them. "Praise God, who has not withdrawn his mercy from the house of Israel," Judith cries, "but has destroyed our enemies by my hand this very night!" (Judith 13:14). She shows the people Holofernes' head and the canopy of the bed. "See here, the head of Holofernes, the commander of the Assyrian army, and here is the canopy beneath which he lay in his drunken stupor. The Lord has struck him down by the hand of a woman. As the Lord lives, who has protected me in the way I went, I swear that it was my face that seduced him to his destruction, and that he committed no sin with me, to defile and shame me" (13:15–16).

Judith has come into her own. She is triumphant.

And yet, this moment also seems to be one of personal struggle. Judith feels a need to proclaim both her victory and, for some reason, her chastity.

Judith might simply be protecting herself against the judgment of law and custom. Because she has not remarried, she is still Manasseh's wife, and to sleep with another man would condemn her to death (see Deuteronomy 22:22). Under the circumstances, however, God and the people of Bethulia would likely forgive her that sin.

Could it be, instead, that Judith is overwhelmed by her own sexuality? She has been grieving deeply. She has only just taken off her widow's garments. She has only just experienced herself again, after many years, as sexually enticing. Someone has crudely lusted for her. Do her words reveal that, deep in her heart, she is not yet ready to imagine herself being physically intimate with someone other than Manasseh?

After beheading Holofernes, Judith leads the Israelites in a crushing defeat of the Assyrians. Her fame spreads, and all the people extol her. "You are the glory of Jerusalem, you are the great boast of Israel, you are the great pride of our nation!" (Judith 15:9). In their eyes she becomes like Moses, a blessed deliverer. Like Moses, she sings a hymn of praise to God, which generations to come, including us, will remember and sing.[4]

Despite the people's adoration, however, and although many men will seek to marry her, Judith never will remarry. Why not?

Feminist interpreters of the Bible today suggest that Judith may enjoy her wealth and independence.[5] Unusual among biblical widows, Judith retains the estate left to her by Manasseh—the gold and silver, slaves, livestock, and fields. She also has plunder from Holofernes, which the Israelites have given to her in thanksgiving for her victory, including the general's silver dishes and furniture. Were she to remarry, all her property would belong to her new husband. We wonder, though, why Judith would not wish to share her good fortune with a husband and children, especially in a society in which marriage is normative and widowhood looked upon with pity.

Is Judith being loyal to Manasseh? In her heart, will Manasseh always be her husband? In the history of Jewish biblical interpretation, this explanation has been popular.[6] Judith, whose Hebrew name (*yehudit*) is the feminine of Judah (*yehudah*), becomes an allegorical personification of the Jewish people. Her fidelity to her husband embodies and encourages the people's faithfulness to God.

Or is it possible that Judith's sexual self has been traumatized? Had she really been ready to take off her widow's garments? For her, doing so seemed sudden, and for anyone to rush into a sexual life can be emotionally painful. The context of a war that links Judith's sexuality to acts of deceit and violence may also cause distress. Judith does not adorn herself for someone she loves, as we would hope for any widow who is rediscovering her beauty and sexuality.

For us, as for Judith, sexuality can be both meaningful and confusing. What is the purpose of our sexuality? Is sexuality good or bad? Do we even feel sexual? Because of our North American culture's expectations about our bodies, and the pervasive depiction of those expectations in our mass media, most of us, at some point, find it a challenge to feel beautiful and sexual. Widows certainly feel those pressures.

Yet widows' feelings about sexuality are even more complex. Because in our society we tend to fear death, we often feel uncomfortable around others who have experienced death. Widows know this social alienation acutely. How can widows feel attractive to others when, on a very real level, people are anxious about being with them?

Widows also must live with the uncertainty, like Judith, of not quite knowing when the relationship with their loved one has truly ended. The death, although very real, is not ultimately what a widow desires or is ready for and, therefore, steals a formal ending. Sometimes, also, widows have experiences of their loved ones after death. So, they wonder: *When, if ever, do I take the photograph out of my wallet? When, if ever, do I take off my ring? Is it okay to wish to feel attractive? Am I ready? Can I possibly ever have sex with anyone else? Will I be hurt? Will my loved one, whom I still miss, approve?*

Are these similar to the prayers of Judith alone in her tent on the rooftop?

☙❧

Prayer and Meditation

For Widows
- How long were you in mourning? Are you still?
- When you became a widow, did you socialize less? If yes, was it your choice?
- If you wore a ring, have you taken it off?
- Do you ever feel that people know you are a widow just by looking at you?
- Do you feel attractive? beautiful? sexual?

For All
- What do you do to feel attractive? Be honest, and name everything.
- Have you ever used sexuality as a means to an end? What was that like?
- Remember a time when you needed tremendous courage to accomplish something.
- Does God strengthen us against the hands of our enemies? What does that say about God?
- Pray Judith's song.

☙❧

A Song of Judith
Judith 16:13–16

I will sing a new song to my God,
> for you are great and glorious, wonderful in
> strength, invincible.
Let the whole creation serve you,
> for you spoke and all things came into
> being.
You sent your breath and it formed them,
> no one is able to resist your voice.

Mountains and seas are stirred to their depths,
    rocks melt like wax at your presence.
But to those who fear you,
    you continue to show mercy.
No sacrifice, however fragrant, can please you,
    but whoever fears the Lord shall stand in
    your sight for ever.[7]

Jane

During those early heartbreaking months after Prosper died, I clung to all symbols of our marriage. His toiletries I left in place in our bathroom; his robe, a Christmas present from me, remained hanging behind the door. The dress shirt that he had changed out of as he prepared to go for a run the night he died hung in our closet for two years. It was several months before I ventured to take off my wedding band, and then only to put it on a chain around my neck. I have since found out that some women wear their wedding rings long after their husbands have died.

I began to wear his clothing—his familiar Madras plaid shirt, his red felt hat, his favorite leather jacket, even his Burberry raincoat. Pros was a big man, and I had lost weight, down to the size eight I was when I first met him. I must have looked ridiculous, but I persisted. The custom of wearing black for a year probably would have been more socially acceptable than wearing his clothing. But I wasn't a conventional woman, nor did I care how I looked, not for at least nine months. I was grieving; I had lost my life's mate; and I wanted the world to witness my loss. More important, I found comfort in wearing his things; I felt as if he were still with me, his arms still encircling.

My greatest need as a widow was for physical intimacy. I denied my need, pretended it didn't exist. But it emerged, in my dreams, in my journals. Nine months after Pros's death, I wrote that I "often feel on a high, like a woman in love, unable to sleep. Intense deep longings surge up in me. But where is my lover; where is the object of this longing?" My wounded heart and confused body cried out to God: Send me an Adam, a helpmate, a lover.

Surely God didn't expect me to love only God? I wanted my mate, my Pros. But if not him, if I was to hold him only in my dreams, then I began to plead and bargain with God for someone else. I wanted human arms around me, someone to hold me, someone to stroke my face and skin, someone whose voice would fill my ears with words of tenderness and passion.

Conflicted and confused, I eventually did throw myself into a couple of affairs that, though not disastrous, could have been. After that, frightened by my seemingly poor judgment and torn because I still loved and wanted my husband, I simply turned off and wore for many years a "Not Available" sign. Good men, available men, were never encouraged. I was always measuring them against Prosper. In death Pros had become almost Godlike, his all-too-human frailties forgotten in my desperate need to immortalize him. And, in my efforts to remain faithful and safely coupled, I, too, was reaching for sainthood.

When a man, perhaps a close friend or Pros's brother, Will, whose hugs were as big and strong as Pros's, would reach out to hold me, I would always be the one to pull away first. Afraid that he, or a watching wife, could see my hunger and would discover my ugly secret—that I longed to be held. I wanted a man's strong arms around me; I wanted kisses and physical intimacy. But I couldn't let go of the image of myself as faithful and loving wife, faithful even in death. And I still loved Pros, still dreamed of him, still missed him. How could I ever think of replacing him? I was in a quandary.

In one heart-stopping instant, I had been suddenly, irrevocably changed, and months later I was still reeling, still off-balance. One moment I was a beloved wife, the mother of his children. I was chosen, the woman he came home to, shared a bed with. I was a woman desired, worthy of hugs, kisses, and intimate whisperings. The next moment I was a widow, my husband lying dead of a heart attack in an emergency room, a John Doe. The world expected me to be lonely and bereft. And I was. I was all of it, lonely and heartbroken, no longer part of a couple, Pros and Jane.

And yet . . .

What was not talked about, what *I* didn't talk about, what I dared not say to anyone except to God, was that in addition to the loneliness, the physical need, the fear, the desolation—in addition to all the expected—*I was also free.* In the silence of a heart no longer beating, in a breath suddenly not taken, I was made a widow, and I was free. At age forty-two I was an adult woman on my own for the first time, with two children to raise. The enormity of this sudden responsibility was heart stopping, and it was exhilarating.

I had a new identity. No longer part of a couple, I was Jane, a widow and a single parent. With or without my wedding ring, with or without his clothing, I was not simply an unmarried woman. I had Pros's legacy of love, and I had our children to give me identity and purpose. I also had his Social Security benefits, a job of my own, a good home in a neighborhood I loved, and a close and supportive Church community. I was secure, whether I believed it or not.

A widow supporting two small children, I was suddenly forced to make my own decisions. I was free to succeed or fail. Free to wear tight sweaters if I chose. "Free to be me" as the sixties song went. Oh, I cowered and quailed, protested and equivocated; decision making is not something that comes easy to me, even now. But I eventually owned the decisions, made them, and I grew. In addition to raising two daughters, I raised myself, or perhaps God raised me. I blossomed, I smiled, and I walked with God. I was free to throw out boxes of Pros's "collections"—I called them "clutter." I paid the bills and marshaled our resources. I blew the dust off my driver's license, rented a car, and drove us to northeastern Connecticut to visit his mother ("Grandma Lucy" to my girls), no longer depending on friends and family to take us. Trembling, praying every mile of the way, I braved Brooklyn-Queens Expressway traffic and the Triboro Bridge, and whizzed up I-95. I got us lost, and I found our way again.

As grief and loneliness shared space in my heart with the glorious joy of being alive and on my own, I reached for another level of independence—I cut my hair. Moreover, I gave Jordan permission to have her long, silky blond tresses cut, for the first time in her life. Pros, although an almost perfect man in many ways, one of the first men I knew to address all women as "Ms.," always an advocate for justice, Pros liked long hair on women. He felt personally betrayed if I even suggested that Jordan or I would like to cut off some of our long and cumbersome hair. That summer, following the second anniversary of Pros's death, I wrote this poem:

July 1990

"And what shall we do today," asked the hairdresser
Her hands poised at the back of my neck
Scissors ready.
Reflected in the mirror
My hair—my pride and joy—chin length, maybe
     longer.
"Just cut the bangs, shape the rest"
The words formed on my tongue.
What came out was—"I want it short."

"What made you decide to have it short?" she
     asked
As her scissors with a will of their own snipped
     away—
My first warning of just how short it was to be.
I smiled serenely, hair falling into my lap.
"I feel like a change" came my reply.

Eighteen years ago we were married, he and I
Our picture sits by my bed.
My hair was long, down my back
"Golden rays of sunshine" he called it.
It was many years before I found courage to cut it
To shed the young self I had outgrown.
I don't believe he ever forgave me—
For growing
For changing.

Now as I lie down to sleep

Alone in our big bed these past two years
I reach back to free the ponytail
Shake out the tangles.
There is no ponytail!

Combing my fingers through the soft fur cap
Of my hair I pause,
The huge gaping hole torn from my heart the night
he died
Is filling up now
Growing into a well
From which I draw the depths of me
The deep golden rays of sunshine
Depths of me.

Anne

Judith, a childless widow like me, is depicted in the Bible as a beautiful, powerful, wise woman. She is so influential and self-possessed that it is hard for me to think of myself as anything like her. A little over a year after David's death, I am only beginning the process of discovering what beauty, power, and wisdom I might have at this new stage of my life.

Beauty? I spent my first year of widowhood looking like lukewarm hell. I was miserable, and my misery showed. There were dark shadows under my eyes. It was a waste of time to apply any makeup because I would just cry it off again before long. Dealing with my hair also seemed like too much trouble, so I didn't even bother to get it cut; I just pulled the back of it into an elastic band and carelessly trimmed the front whenever it threatened to obstruct my vision.

The garments of my mourning were drab items that had been in my closet before David became ill. Most of these clothes either didn't fit properly or had gone out of style. During the year after his death, I regained some of the weight I'd lost during the terror and stress of his illness, but I was almost never in any mood to go shopping for better-fitting choices. On the rare occasions when I did venture into cloth-ing stores, most of what I tried on seemed frivolous and somehow irrelevant to the life I was living. I had some interesting jewelry, but the only pieces I felt like wearing were my wedding rings and the gold-and-silver ring David bought me from a mail-order catalog shortly before he died. Without a job to go to any longer, there were fewer incentives to dress up and make an effort to look better. This way of presenting myself felt protective, rather like armor; it enabled me to fade into the background, to hide. To mourn without attracting attention. To look as sad on the outside as I felt on the inside. When I complimented people on how they looked, I was thankful that they were always kind enough to refrain from saying anything about how I looked.

Once the anniversary of David's death had passed, though, there began to be times when I felt like I was starting to climb out from under the heavy weight of grief. There were increasingly long stretches when that weight didn't feel quite so heavy. My energy level began to rise. And then came moments when I even cared about how I looked.

At about that time, I bought a sweater that actually fit me, and I found it cheered me up immensely. My weight had finally stabilized, and I was getting tired of looking so forlorn. It felt like the time had come for me to move beyond the mourning garments. David was always pleased when I got new clothes, and at that point I could almost hear him saying to me, "Stop crying now, and go shopping!"

Recently I took an important step. A long-divorced friend of mine was remarrying, and I was invited to her wedding. Before the occasion several of our friends were comparing notes about what they intended to wear. Staring dejectedly into a mirror, I doubted it would ever be possible for me to feel good about how I looked again. Was I too old now even to be concerned with that? Was it time for me to acknowledge that that phase of my life was over?

For the first year after he died, David almost never appeared in my dreams. But the night after the conversation with my friends, I dreamed I was attending a relative's wedding in a synagogue that had many beautiful, ornate rooms. The ceremony was to be performed by the rabbi who had conducted David's funeral. All of a sudden, David showed up to join me! He was well and whole, and everyone seemed quite matter-of-fact about his being there, even though it was known that he had died. Eventually, because the rabbi was so late in arriving, David started leading us toward the door. I told him I wasn't ready to leave yet, so we stayed and talked about photography for the rest of the dream. It was delightful to have him with me again!

I am no expert on dream interpretation, but I do know I awoke energized and confident that it was finally time to do something about my appearance. I strode into the nearest haircutting shop and emerged with my hair many inches shorter and styled in a way that I thought looked distinctly better. Dressing up for the wedding that weekend, I decided it wasn't time for me to give up on feeling attractive quite yet.

I am not likely to stop wearing my wedding band or my three-diamond anniversary ring anytime soon, however. When David was alive I never removed those rings except to clean them. They are the most important and cherished pieces of jewelry I have ever owned, and going around without them still seems unthinkable. I am not married anymore, but I am not available either. My sexuality is still so blunted by mourning and menopause that I haven't felt attracted to anyone. I suppose a time may come when I would be open to the possibility of a new relationship and would feel like taking off the rings. Or perhaps I might start by wearing David's last gift to me, the gold-and-silver ring, on that finger instead. But that would be in the hard-to-imagine future. For now, the wedding rings stay on.

Power? One thing I have found unexpectedly engaging has been learning how to do the things David used to do around the house. During the months when he had back pain but could still walk, he'd made a point of showing me how to take care of tasks such as resetting circuit breakers and draining and replacing the water in the boiler, and I'd made a point of paying attention. Not long after he died, a pipe in the basement developed a serious leak. After the plumber made the repair, I asked him to show me how to deal with other potential problems (shutting down valves, checking the pilot light in the water heater, adjusting the flushometer). As I had done with David, I followed the plumber around the house and took notes.

My husband liked tools, and he left me with an excellent supply of them. I don't know how to use them all yet, but I am learning, task by task. These days, when something in the house breaks, springs a leak, or quits working, my first response is still to cry and get angry because I don't know what to do and he isn't here to take care of it. This response can overtake me suddenly and with considerable intensity. I attacked my malfunctioning printer with a screwdriver; I punched my fist through a screen that I couldn't manage to remove from a window. But after letting off some steam, I am usually able to dry my eyes, take several deep breaths, remind myself that I'm not helpless, and try to approach the problem in some sort of reasonable way. Every time I figure out how to fix a stuck door, replace the battery in the alarm system, or install an air conditioner in the window, I feel especially close to David. I like to think that his power to take care of our physical environment is in some way becoming part of me.

Wisdom? I think grief must have affected my cognitive processes in some way. There have been many occasions during my bereavement when it seemed I could barely remember my own name, let alone anyone else's. I have arrived at stores with no recollection whatsoever of what I'd gone there to buy. I have dialed phone numbers and then forgotten why I called by the time the person answered. I have had trouble coming up with coherent responses in conversations. I have stuttered, mumbled, and gasped as my sluggish brain searched for words to express an idea. I have felt confused and stupid more times than I can count.

Before David died I wrote a book about spiritual direction. Recently I was invited to present, with a colleague, a short continuing-education course on the topic of my book. For weeks before the course began, I worried about whether I had recovered enough to be up to the task. Would I be able to sound like I knew what I was talking about under the pressure of a new teaching situation? Would I find myself flipping frantically through my own book in front of the class, trying to recall what I'd written? I warned my colleague that he might have to step in for me whenever I lost my train of thought.

Fortunately, my fears were largely unfounded. Even though my thinking is still fairly jumbled, the course went well, I was able to remember most of what I needed to remember, and eventually I was even able to relax enough to have a good time. Like Judith, I had devoted considerable time to prayer in the days that led up to the event. Doing so, I felt more like the Moses of Exodus 4:10 ("but I am slow of speech and slow of tongue") than the eloquent and confident Judith of Judith 9:9 ("Give to me, a widow, the strong hand to do what I plan"). I may not have spoken wisely during the class that followed, but at least I was able to speak relatively sensibly. I continue to have trouble expressing myself in speech, and words like *widow* stick so tightly in my throat that I can't even pronounce them sometimes. But the experience of teaching the class made an impression on me nonetheless. Could it be that trust in God is the beginning of wisdom?

chapter eight

❊

Ruth

The Book of Ruth

THE FIRST UNACCOMPANIED WORDS FROM RUTH are her vow. With Orpah she had offered, on the road from Moab to Bethlehem, to continue journeying with their mother-in-law, Naomi. By returning to Naomi's childhood home, they might find compassion and provision. Soon, in response to Naomi's urgent plea for the sake of her daughters-in-law, Orpah changes her mind and returns home to her own family and gods in Moab. Yet Ruth clings to Naomi, and we hear Ruth's pure voice proclaiming with beauty, sorrow, and strength a promise to Naomi of lifelong companionship:

> Where you go, I will go;
>   where you lodge, I will lodge;
> your people shall be my people,
>   and your God my God.
> Where you die, I will die—
>   there will I be buried.
> *(Ruth 1:16–17)*

Ruth's words are eloquent, her emotions powerful, her vow sincere.

This poignant moment reveals an often unrecognized grief for new widows—the loss of covenant relationship.

A grace of being human is our ability to live in relationships of love and fidelity and to vow to do so. In our contemporary North American culture, it is said, we have become
reticent to make commitments to one another. Self-interest,
anxiety, and an obsession with defining ourselves by accumu-
lating possessions have broken our sense of interconnection,
communion, and responsibility for one another. We find it
difficult to make promises to others, especially lifelong vows.
Deep down, however, our natural human yearning is to live
in covenant relationships of mutual fidelity, respect, and
care. By doing so, we can become our true selves in the image
of God. For again and again in Scripture, God shows *chesed,*
a Hebrew word meaning "steadfast love," to the people to
whom God has promised faithfulness. When we make promises of steadfast love to one another, we express our desire to
be holy, our belief in life and love, our hope for the future,
and our trust in God. When we keep our promises and, like
God, abound in steadfast love, we are most like the selves
God created us to be.

Like all new widows, Ruth knows the joy of having lived
in covenant relationship and the immediate, terrible loss of
that grace. Her husband Mahlon, Naomi's son, has just died.
Although the first part of the Book of Ruth focuses on
Naomi's bitter sorrow at having lost her husband and two
sons, undoubtedly Ruth's grief is also profound. Like Naomi,
Ruth mourns the death of a husband and, because she is
childless, faces a dire economic future. Perhaps even more
sharply, she feels the pain of lost promise. To whom can she
now be committed and faithful? As some new widows might,
she cannot promise to love and take care of her children
always. To whom can she show steadfast love?

Ruth's human need to be in covenant relationship, as well
as her affection for Naomi, may inspire her tender promise to
befriend Naomi always. The words of her vow are similar to
the promises a spouse or lifelong lover would make: "I will
love you, comfort you, honor and keep you, in sickness and
in health, and be faithful to you as long as we both shall
live."[1] As Ruth speaks her vow, she *clings* to Naomi (see
Ruth 1:14), the closest physical bond between two women in

all of Scripture. The moment thus resonates with the ideal of marriage presented in the Genesis creation story, "Therefore a man leaves his father and his mother and clings to his wife" (Genesis 2:24). In a very real sense, Naomi is becoming Ruth's new lifelong partner, the object of Ruth's *chesed*, or steadfast love. Ruth even fervently avows that this new relationship with Naomi will last beyond the grave, a promise that may reveal Ruth's inner fear of losing covenant relationship yet again: "May the Lord do thus and so to me, / and more as well, / if even death parts me from you!" (Ruth 1:17).

Ruth's exquisite vow comes in a moment of intense anguish, loss, and grief. She is mourning Mahlon's death, bidding farewell to her sister-in-law, Orpah, and leaving behind her homeland and family. Nevertheless, her words are not a rash, impassioned mistake that she later rescinds. For the rest of her life, Ruth will keep her promise. She will offer something her mother-in-law desperately needs—abiding friendship—even in the face of embarrassment and sacrifice. Thereby, Ruth, whose name means "friendship," will be able to be her true self, living a holy and committed life.

After they arrive together in Bethlehem and Naomi greets her childhood friends, an immediate task for mother-in-law and daughter-in-law is to find food. Because of the law allowing widows and sojourning foreigners to glean the agricultural fields for wheat, barley, grapes, and other left-behind produce, Ruth, who is both a widow and a foreigner, offers to glean in the fields of Bethlehem. Naomi agrees, yet does not go with her to the fields. Perhaps Naomi is too old to withstand the physical demands of gleaning. Perhaps she is too embarrassed to be seen in her hometown in the shameful social position of widowhood. Perhaps she is too worn down by grief to find enough energy to do work. So Ruth gleans for them both, putting herself at some risk of being ridiculed or even harmed because she is a foreigner from a hostile neighboring country, a widow, and a young woman out in the world alone.

By chance Ruth gleans in the field of Boaz, a relative of Naomi's. Boaz is curious about Ruth and learns from his reapers that she is the Moabite woman who has returned with Naomi to Bethlehem. Then, calling her "my daughter" (Ruth 2:8), Boaz invites Ruth to glean only in his field and to help herself to water from his well when she becomes thirsty. He commands his young men not to bother her. When Ruth expresses surprise at his generosity, Boaz explains that he is aware of the steadfast love she has shown to Naomi. "All that you have done for your mother-in-law since the death of your husband has been fully told me, and how you left your father and mother and your native land and came to a people you did not know before. May the Lord reward you for your deeds, and may you have a full reward from the Lord, the God of Israel, under whose wings you have come for refuge!" (Ruth 2:11–12). At the noon meal, Boaz invites Ruth to eat with his reapers and offers her enough parched grain to satisfy her hunger, with some left over to take home to Naomi. Then, as the reaping begins again, he instructs his young men to pull handfuls of grain from the gathered bundles for her to glean.

On seeing the unexpectedly large amount of food Ruth brings home, Naomi questions where she has gleaned. Learning that Ruth had worked in the field of Boaz, she suddenly realizes that he, as a kinsman, might be even more generous by serving as a *go'el*, a Hebrew word meaning "one with the right to redeem," often translated as "next-of-kin." Because Naomi's sons have died, she cannot arrange a Levirate marriage for Ruth, thereby ensuring that Elimelech's name will "not be blotted out of Israel" should Ruth then bear a son and heir (Deuteronomy 25:6). But Naomi might be able to stay connected to Elimelech's property in Bethlehem and therefore offer herself and Ruth some economic security. A male relative could serve as *go'el* by redeeming a piece of land sold by a family member under economic duress, thus ensuring that the property would remain within the family (see Leviticus 25:25).

With this new possibility, Naomi asks Ruth to make an even greater sacrifice than she has already. "Now wash and anoint yourself, and put on your best clothes and go down to the threshing floor;[2] but do not make yourself known to the man until he has finished eating and drinking. When he lies down, observe the place where he lies; then, go and uncover his feet and lie down; and he will tell you what to do" (Ruth 3:3–4). In the biblical world, the word *feet* was a euphemism for a man's genitals. Naomi is asking Ruth to try to seduce Boaz.

To do so will be risky and deeply embarrassing for Ruth. Law and custom condemned extramarital sex, and when a man slept with another man's wife, both were to be sentenced to death (Deuteronomy 22:22). Until she remarries, Ruth is still Mahlon's wife. To seduce Boaz, meanwhile, will recall in her heart the shameful story among the Israelites about the beginning of her own people, the Moabites. According to the story, when the patriarch Abraham's nephew, Lot, had lost his home and wife in the destruction of Sodom, he fled to a cave with his two daughters. Anxious about not having children, his daughters over two nights made Lot drunk with wine and seduced him. Both daughters became pregnant by this incest, and the oldest daughter named her son Moab, who became the ancestor of all Moabites (see Genesis 19:30–37). Not only does Ruth know this tale, but also Boaz has treated her as a father, just as Lot was a father to his daughters; Boaz has fed and protected her and called her "my daughter." At best, even if Boaz does delight in her and agrees to marry her, Ruth realizes the townspeople of Bethlehem may always socially shun her, simply because she is a foreigner.

Nevertheless, Ruth will keep her vow. She will care for Naomi, putting her mother-in-law's well-being ahead of her own. "All that you tell me," she promises Naomi, "I will do" (Ruth 3:5).

Fortunately, Boaz, a man of God, redeems the situation. After having fallen contentedly asleep at the edge of the grain heap, he is startled awake at midnight to find Ruth lying at his feet and asking him to spread his cloak over her, for he is a potential *go'el*. She is not simply asking Boaz to enjoy sex with her. She is requesting marriage, for to spread your *cloak* (*kenaphecha*) would be, according to Hebrew custom, to propose marriage, which would offer Ruth protection under God's *wings* (*kenaphav*), as Boaz has already prayed for

her.[3] Immediately Boaz recognizes the sacrifice she is making
and the loyalty she is showing to Naomi. "May you be blessed
by the LORD, my daughter; this last instance of your loyalty
(*chesed*) is better than the first; you have not gone after
young men, whether poor or rich" (Ruth 3:10). Boaz sees
that Ruth has left behind her homeland, her family, and the
possibility of remarrying in Moab. To find security for Naomi,
she has risked danger in the grain fields and shame and condemnation on the threshing floor. She has endeavored to
find a husband among men discouraged from marrying foreign women. She has even accepted the possibility of someday becoming a widow again by not seeking to marry a
younger man. Touched by her sacrifice and steadfast love for
Naomi, Boaz agrees to help Ruth in every way he can.

Boaz first protects Ruth's reputation and their social standing by sending her home before dawn, so that she will not
be discovered. She carries with her more grain. The next day
Boaz meets with elders of Bethlehem to ensure social acceptance of his marriage to Ruth. Naomi has another male
relative more closely related than Boaz who, therefore, has
the right to redeem Elimelech's property before Boaz. In the
gathering of men, Boaz tells this kinsman about Ruth and
cleverly links her to the property. The kinsman declines to
serve as the *go'el*. With the blessing of elders and the townspeople, Boaz agrees both to redeem the property and to marry
Ruth; by this public negotiation, he has won the community's acceptance of Ruth to be his wife. He is a redeemer in
every sense.

Ruth and Boaz marry and soon have a son, whom the
women of the neighborhood name Obed. He is to become
the father of Jesse, who will be the father of King David.
Obed is also Naomi's grandson, who will secure her future
and bring her joy. Naomi's women friends in Bethlehem
gather around her to praise God for Naomi's restored fortune.
They give thanks for Ruth, who, they tell Naomi, "loves you,
who is more to you than seven sons" (Ruth 4:15). In Judaism,
seven is a number signifying wholeness. Because of Ruth's
steadfast love, Naomi is now whole. She had left Bethlehem
with Elimelech in a time of famine, her belly empty. After

the deaths of her husband and sons, she had returned to her childhood home with an empty heart. Now she is full, belly and heart.

In making her marriage vow to Boaz, Ruth keeps her life-long vow to Naomi. She has befriended her mother-in-law through great suffering and, by her faithfulness, restored both Naomi and herself to new life.

Are we willing, like Ruth, to overcome embarrassment and social risk to offer friendship to widows and other people in need? When we are in need ourselves, are we able to accept the friendship of others, even sacrificial friendship? Do we, like Ruth, yearn to make commitments to others? Can we find creative ways to make such commitments, beyond traditional social institutions such a marriage between a man and a woman? To whom will we cling with steadfast love?

☙〜◉

Prayer and Meditation

For Widows
- Remember the vows you made to your loved one.
- After the death, did you still feel bound by your promises?
- Do you yearn to make a commitment to someone else? Have you already?
- When you became a widow, who befriended you? Did their friendship help?
- Are you able to reach out in friendship to other widows?
- Light a candle in thanksgiving for the grace and power God has given you to make commitments of friendship and love, and then pray Psalm 116.

For All
- Is making a lifelong vow easy or difficult for you?
- Pray Psalm 61:4–5.
- When someone else is hurting, do you tend to feel uncomfortable and turn away, or do you reach out in friendship?

- Have you ever done something emotionally hard for the sake of someone else? Tell God about the sacrifice you made.
- If you have ever cared for an aging parent, remember all your feelings.
- In a quiet place, gaze on a crucifix and reflect on Jesus' sacrifice.
- This very day, promise to do something tangible and generous for someone you love. Name the act in your heart, and then honor your commitment.

❂❀❂

Anne

When I think back on how miserable I was in the months after David's death and how difficult it was for me to interact with other people, I sometimes wonder: What *did* I wish people would do? How *did* I want to be treated?

Judging from my experience, it seems that when we are bereaved, we can be sad, confused, and angry, all at the same time. Trying to comfort us might be like trying to hug a porcupine: when we are hurting, getting close to us can hurt, too. Or perhaps it is like walking across a minefield: it is difficult to know which attempts to be helpful will spark a negative reaction (such as my prickly responses to the question, "How are you?"). Looking back, I think I was unable to articulate my needs because I didn't even know what they were. The only thing I remember wanting for sure was for somebody to bring David back—which was, of course, the one thing no one could do for me.

Short of bringing David back, however, there were a variety of things people did that gave me some comfort. Friends and colleagues, including many whom I had not seen in years or didn't expect to hear from, called or wrote to me. For weeks I kept the entire collection of sympathy cards, letters, e-mails, and charity-contribution notifications spread out across the dining-room table. I would sit there and read through them again and again, marveling at the variety of ways people expressed their condolences and caring. I'm sure those who have lost a loved one differ greatly with respect to what helps them, but I know I especially appreciated it when people:

- told me what they liked and admired about David
- indicated that they could see how much we loved each other (his co-workers described how his face would light up when he talked about me)
- acknowledged my care of him ("He was blessed indeed to have you with him throughout his illness and during those last hours")
- made charitable contributions in his memory
- brought meals to me, came over to eat take-out food with me, or invited me out to eat
- offered to accompany me to places where I was reluctant to go by myself (Jeanne went with me to David's favorite diner, where people asked how he was and I had to tell them he had died)
- phoned or emailed to keep in touch
- told me what they had found helpful in similar situations (from Jane: "I remember that one thing I really needed was to be alone to mourn and to be with God. But sometimes it was a relief to have friends step in and do some tasks")
- said they believed David was safe in God's care

"Accept every invitation you get during the first year," my friend Natalie advised me early in my bereavement. At the time I thought she meant I should keep busy in an effort to ward off sadness. I didn't follow her advice to the letter, mostly because it sounded too strenuous. But now I wonder whether that suggestion might have been about more than just keeping busy: Perhaps it was also about the importance of community in getting through grief.

Even though I often wished to curl up and hide, or felt too cranky to reach out to anybody, the undeniable reality was—and continues to be—that I need other people. In the wake of David's death, I needed to be in situations where I could relax and be myself without having to worry about whether I

was burdening anybody with my unhappiness. I needed to be
with people who would acknowledge my feelings and be sym-
pathetic without trying to "fix" me. I needed people to help
me keep from sinking into inactivity and to remind me that
there were still things in life that were interesting and worth-
while. Especially, I needed to feel that there were people to
whom it mattered whether I lived or died. No one could take
away my inevitable sorrow, but at least they could make me
feel accepted, held, and cared for while I endured it.

Reading the story of Ruth and Naomi, I am impressed by
the loyalty and mutual support the two women demonstrate
in the face of famine, geographic dislocation, illness, and
death. After their husbands die, Ruth decides they must stay
together and help each other survive. As a result of Naomi's
guidance and family connections, Ruth eventually ends up
with a new husband and a son, Naomi gets "a restorer of life
and a nourisher of [her] old age," and both get financial security. During the early months of my own widowhood, I found
myself feeling envious of the dramatic reversal of fortune they
experienced. How wonderful it would be, I thought, if someone, or some community, would show up and be "more to
[me] than seven sons" (Ruth 4:15). But how likely was that?

What I eventually discovered was that, although no community provided everything I needed, there were a number of
communities within my reach that each had something to
offer. For me those communities were friends, family, the
Ruth and Naomi Circle at Grace Church, the twelve-
step recovery program I recently joined, and a group of my
spiritual-direction colleagues who meet for peer supervision
and support. Like Ruth and Naomi, I often had to be deliberate about identifying what I wanted and about making an
effort to move toward it. I had to push against the pressure of
my inertia, my introversion, and my need to "act okay." It has
not been easy, but it has been worth the effort.

More than a year after David's death, my struggle with
grief continues. I still think of him with longing and cry at
unpredictable times. I still write letters to him, especially in
connection with special occasions and important decisions. I
still feel disoriented and off-balance in many situations. I still

experience unsettling flashes of anger. I still find it exceedingly hard to ask for help. My ability to relate to the rest of the world is still a work in progress.

Lately, though, I have noticed that the events leading up to David's death don't replay in my mind as often as they once did. I am beginning to think of him in a more balanced way, to remember him as he was throughout all the years we were together. I am regaining my ability to see him not as a perfect, flawless hero, but as a regular human being with many qualities I liked and a few I didn't like so much. I am trying to incorporate what I admired about him into myself. And I think I must be feeling better, because my responses when people ask me how I am have changed considerably:

Question: *How are you?*
Answer 1:   *Better than last year, thanks.*
Answer 2:   *I feel like I'm starting to climb out from under a rock!*
Answer 3:   *I still miss David so much, but I think he'd be pleased with how well I'm managing.*
Answer 4:   *I have good days and bad days. So far, this is a good (or bad) day.*
Answer 5:   (on a bad day, to someone I don't know well) *It's hard to say at the moment.*
Answer 6:   (on a bad day, to someone I know well) *Bereavement bites!*
Answer 7:   *Thank you for asking, and for caring about me!*

The two years recently past—the year of David's illness and the year following his death—have been the most difficult in my life. Never before have I felt so broken, terrified, drained, inundated, or weighed down. No longer do I live each day with someone who understands and cherishes me the way he did. As the difficult memories of his final months begin to fade, there are times now when I wonder whether grief might be the main thing that still connects me to him. Will I lose my ability to recall his face or voice without the aid of the photos I keep all over the house or the videotape our granddaughter Lillian made at a family gathering a few years ago? Will I be able to move beyond sadness as a way of clinging to him?

Ruth makes the choice to leave behind everything that is familiar in order to accompany Naomi to Bethlehem. Presumably she doesn't forget about her life in Moab with Mahlon, as if it were no longer important to her. But she does move on. And I know David would want me to move on, too.

Even so, it is not easy. Most of his clothing remains in the closet. His eyeglasses, wristwatch, keys, pocket change, and green sweater still sit on top of his dresser. His toothbrush continues to occupy its usual place next to mine in the holder over the sink. If he were to come back, he would have no trouble finding anything he needed. It is immensely difficult for me to let go of the well-known and beloved terrain of the life we shared.

They say God reaches us and transforms us through our broken places. I certainly have plenty of broken places for God to work with now. But I have survived so far, and I think I've grown. There are even times when I can say I have been fortunate. I had David to love for twenty-four years. I learned that I can do things I never imagined I was capable of doing. There are people in my life who care about me. With the help of God and community, I hope to continue to grow.

There is a time to mourn, and there is a time to dance. I hope someday to dance again.

Jane

My parents were the first people I called in those early hours of the morning after Prosper's death. My father answered. "Daddy," I whispered into the phone, "Pros is dead." I could hear my mother in the background asking anxiously, "Willie, what is it? What's wrong?" A telephone ringing at 5:00 a.m. does not usually bring good news, at least not in our family. Birth and wedding announcements waited for decent hours; death was more importunate.

I had been up all night, waiting, waiting to tell them—my family, his family, the children, and our friends—waiting to share my grief, waiting for them to close ranks around us, to hold us up with their love and care. My brother called back an hour or so later to say he and my father would both be on a plane soon and arrive that afternoon. My mother wasn't well and was going to stay at home.

Fortunately, my close friends in the prayer group at Grace Church had already begun walking with me in my new journey into widowhood. They had been waiting for me to join them the night before, the night Pros died. As I ran into the room crying, "Something is dreadfully wrong, Pros is not home yet," they were gathered around the piano, singing our favorite "old" hymns. Quickly they followed me home, telling me what to do, helping with the children, making phone calls, and praying. One of them spent the night. So when the morning dawned, I was not alone.

People cope with their losses, their tragedies, in different ways. I coped because God was with me through people. I needed people, friends, family. I even sought and received comfort from strangers, something that used to mystify and embarrass my children. I needed people, I needed their touch, their hugs, their voices of caring, their smiles, their tears of empathy. In those early days, food appeared in my house and neighbors answered my phone, took messages, and received condolences. A friend was always with me, with us. If I wanted to go to Connecticut to be with Pros's family, someone would offer to drive. A friend told me about the Social Security benefits for the children and then accompanied me, sat with me, helped with the questions and forms.

When I needed to talk, needed to feel secure and cared for, I knew I could call my priest, a friend, or a neighbor. Numbly, I stumbled through those early weeks, engulfed by grief and confusion, but knowing on some deep level that I and the girls were cared for. A protective circle of comfort and support surrounded us. At the time I simply accepted the love and support, only occasionally remembering to say thank you. Now I see all their faces, some who are no longer around, and I am moved to tears and deep gratitude.

A few days after the funeral, as my father and brother were preparing to return home to Tennessee, my father drew me aside. He confessed in his slow mountain drawl that they had come to comfort and help, yes, but also to "fetch me home"—children, belongings, everything. "Your Mama said to bring you home." "Except," he continued, his steady blue eyes locked onto mine, "we realized after spending some time with you and the girls that you have more community here than we have in Tennessee." Matching his drawl, I allowed as how this strange, alien Yankee city to which Pros had brought me had become my home. I would stay.

It is true that God can't put arms around you, God can't cook a meal for hungry children, and God can't drive you to visit your family. But God's people can and did. God's people cared for us and bound our broken family into community.

To those who stop me with "I don't know how you have done it, managed so well. You are so strong," I have now lived into an answer. My reply is simple: I called on God, and I called on God's people, and they heard my cry. As the psalmist says, "On the day I called, you answered me, / you increased my strength of soul" (Psalm 138:3).[4] Any strength I have within me comes from God and grows in community.

epilogue

❧

Widows and Saints

Acts 9:36–42

THE LIFE-GIVING FRIENDSHIP OF WIDOWS is what we hope, most of all, to offer you. So, as we close our book, we invite you to glean from one more story. It is a miracle story in which a gathering of unnamed widows seems an insignificant detail. Nevertheless, the presence of the widows expresses what we have discovered to be true—that widows' companionship is, for everyone, a gift of renewal and promise.

The story is about Peter's emergence as a Christian leader among the Gentiles. Jesus has died, returned to life, and departed to be with God forever. Now, the disciples are suddenly left truly alone to spread the good news of what they have experienced and to carry on Jesus' ministry of teaching, healing, and miracle-making.

One day, when Peter is fulfilling this mission in Lydda, west of Jerusalem, messengers arrive from Joppa, a nearby city on the coast of the Mediterranean Sea, to request his help. Peter goes with them at once and, upon arrival in Joppa, is taken to an upper room. Here lies the body of Tabitha (whose Greek name is Dorcas), a disciple who has died.[1]

Surrounding her are all the widows of the city. When Peter enters, the widows stand beside him, weeping. They show him things that tell him about Tabitha. We can hear their memories: *She was very talented. Look, here are tunics she sewed while she was with us. Though most people shun us because we are widows, she spent time with us. She was generous to us. She gave us clothing to wear. Everyone in the city knows of her good works and almsgiving. She made this garment, too. We miss her.*

For our Ruth and Naomi Circles at Grace Church, we often, like the grieving widows, would bring in something tangible that called forth memories. One of us might bring in a photograph, a beloved book, a handwritten letter, a hat. We passed around whatever the item was so that each of us could hold it, as we listened to our sister-widow tell us something about the one who had died.

Soon Peter asks the widows of Joppa to go outside the upper room. Alone with Tabitha's body, he kneels and prays. Then, turning toward her, he tells her to rise. She opens her eyes. Beholding Peter, she sits up. When he takes her by the hand, she stands. It is a miracle worthy to be proclaimed. Calling all "the saints and widows" of Joppa as witnesses, Peter shows Tabitha to be alive (Acts 9:41).

Peter is a miracle worker in the tradition of Elijah, Elisha, and Jesus, all of whom also raised people from physical death.[2] Unlike these servants of God, we are not miracle workers. We cannot free David, or Prosper, or the departed loved ones of our Ruth and Naomi sisters, or anyone else from the tangible cords of death. This is not the kind of resurrection we can offer.

Instead, we see ourselves in the widows surrounding Tabitha. We can help, as they did, to bring about new life— if not a physical resurrection, then a spiritual one.

In writing this book, we have discovered the saving health of praying our stories in parallel with the stories of other widows. As we have befriended one another, and the biblical widows, we have gained new hope for both ourselves and our loved ones who have died. Remembering in community has brought our loved ones back to life for us in a way we would not have otherwise known. It has brought us back to life, too.

If you are a widow, we hope that you will continue to pray your own story in companionship with us and the widows of the Bible. In our prayer, we will be listening. With friendship, we will remember along with you. Where you go, we shall.

And like the widows who loved Tabitha, we will be waiting just outside the upper room for you, and just outside the tomb of your loved one, to behold a new beginning.

No matter who you are, this book is our gift to you. In the story of Tabitha, Peter calls not just the grieving widows but all the saints of Joppa to see Tabitha alive again. Similarly, God invites you, as one of the saints, to witness resurrection life in the company of widows. You have graciously accepted this holy invitation by reading this book.

We believe in the communion of saints. We believe in, and are grateful for, your friendship and love. We believe in the resurrection of the dead. Somehow they are all connected.

notes

Chapter 1: Abigail

1. In later centuries the Jewish Targum, the Aramaic translation of the Hebrew Scriptures, will suggest that Abigail's expression refers to life after death. To this day her words are used in memorial prayers for the dead and as an inscription on tombstones.

2. Scripture includes many stories and images indicating the meaning of completeness in these numbers. Among them, for *seven:* God creates the world in six days and rests on the seventh, establishing the Sabbath (Genesis 1:1–2:4). Jacob works for Laban seven years to win his beloved Rachel as a wife; when Laban tricks Jacob into marriage with Leah instead, Jacob then works another seven years for Rachel (Genesis 29:15–30). The finest silver is refined seven times (Psalm 12:6). For *three:* The created order has three realms—heavens, earth, and underworld. The sanctuary has three parts—vestibule, nave, and inner sanctuary (1 Kings 6:2–22). Jonah lives in the belly of the great fish for three days and three nights (Jonah 1:17). Prayer is encouraged three times each day (Psalm 55:17, Daniel 6:10). For a discussion of the symbolism of these numbers in both the Hebrew Scriptures and the New Testament, see "Numbers," *The HarperCollins Bible Dictionary,* Paul J. Achtemeier et al., eds. (San Francisco: HarperCollins, 1985), 763–764.

Chapter 2: Naomi

1. James E. Griffiss, *Naming the Mystery: How Our Words Shape Prayer and Belief* (Cambridge, MA: Cowley Publications, 1990), 171.

2. Some Jewish thinkers today also seem to struggle with Naomi's initiative to change her own name. In a well-received commentary on the Book of Ruth by contemporary Jewish women, *Reading Ruth*, scholar Nehama Aschkenasy interprets Naomi's imperative to the women of Bethlehem as a creative rhetorical strategy to change not her name but her circumstances: "What Naomi means is, of course, not that her name should be changed, but that her *reality* should be mended and altered to conform to her original name. Naomi's elaborate polemics about her name are meant as a challenge to her own fate, a call to God to adjust her life so that it will once again reflect the true meaning of her name" (115). Although Naomi undoubtedly wishes that her life were different, we cannot imagine her, in this moment of mourning, astutely engaging in such a theological plan of action. She cannot even yet remember her kinsman Boaz, who might extend compassion and help to Naomi and Ruth. Naomi's words, then, are the sincere and heartfelt cry of a deeply grieving widow. See Nehama Aschkenasy, "Language as Female Empowerment in Ruth," *Reading Ruth: Contemporary Women Reclaim a Sacred Story*, Judith A. Kates and Gail Twersky Reimer, eds. (New York: Ballantine Books, 1994), 111–124.

3. In the era of the kings of Judah, Pharoah Neco of Egypt usurps God's authority and relationship with the Judeans by murdering King Josiah, installing a son of Josiah as a puppet king, and changing the son's name from Eliakim to Jehoiakim (2 Kings 23:34). A few years later, King Nebuchadnezzar of Babylon does the same by overtaking Judah from Egypt, bringing Israelites into exile, teaching them the language and literature of the Chaldeans, and changing their names. Among the exiles is Daniel, whom

King Nebuchadnezzar names Betleshazzar (Daniel 1:6–7). By these acts, Pharoah Neco and King Nebuchadnezzar try to take the place of God. In the Christian story, Jesus changes Simon's name to Peter (Matthew 16:18, Luke 6:14), manifesting, according to the gospel authors, the presence, power, and authority of God within Jesus.

4. Barbara Cawthorne Crafton, *The Sewing Room* (New York: Viking, 1993), 238–239.

Chapter 3: The Widow of Zarephath

1. From the opening words of the liturgy for the Celebration and Blessing of a Marriage in *The Book of Common Prayer* (1979), 423.

2. Lisa Belcher Hamilton, *For Those We Love But See No Longer: Daily Offices for Times of Grief* (Brewster, MA: Paraclete Press, 2001), 99.

Chapter 4: The Widow with Two Coins

1. A compelling argument that Jesus is making a critique of the Temple economy, rather than telling a pronouncement story about the widow's piety, is given by Addison G. Wright, "The Widow's Mites: Praise or Lament," *Catholic Biblical Quarterly*, 44.2 (1982), 256–265.

2. *Forward Day By Day*, 69:3 (August–October 2003), 23.

Chapter 5: Tamar

1. Rainer Maria Rilke, *On Love and Other Difficulties*, trans. by John J. L. Mood (New York: W. W. Norton and Company, 1975), 25.

2. "Saying Kaddish" means reciting a prayer with which Jews memorialize the dead during worship services. Written mostly in Aramaic, its poetic lines do not actually mention death or grief, but rather—like the Lord's Prayer—praise God and look toward the sovereignty of God on earth. See Anita Diamant, *Saying Kaddish: How to Comfort the Dying, Bury the Dead, and Mourn As a Jew* (New York: Schocken Books, 1998), 27.

3. This prayer is chanted or spoken during funerals and visits to graves. It asks God to care for the departed and expresses the wish that his or her soul "be bound up in the bond of eternal life" (Diamant, *Saying Kaddish,* 79). These words echo Abigail's plea to David in 1 Samuel 25:29.

Chapter 6: Anna

1. Luke's Gospel remembers the economic hardship for widows of a severe famine during the time of Elijah (4:25–26); tells of Jesus raising from the dead the only son of a widow at Nain, thereby restoring her economic security (7:11–17); relates Jesus' parable of the persistent widow who seeks justice (18:1–8); notes Jesus' condemnation of Jewish scribes for devouring widows' houses (20:47); and includes the teaching of Jesus based on his observation of a poor widow who gives her last two coins into the Temple treasury (21:1–4).

2. The religious, social, and economic status of Jewish women in the first century CE was diverse. Archaeological and literary sources suggest that, even with a patriarchal society, some Jewish women were landowners and financially independent, while others enjoyed religious education, dedicated their lives to the study of Torah, and even were leaders in synagogues. See Jane Schaberg, "Luke," *The Women's Bible Commentary,* Carol A. Newsom and Sharon H. Ringe, eds. (Louisville, KY: Westminster/John Knox Press, 1992), 279.

3. In the story of Simeon and Anna, three rituals required under Jewish law are conflated into one event—Jesus' circumcision and naming eight days after his birth (Leviticus 12:3), the presentation of the firstborn son at the Temple (Exodus 13:2, Numbers 18:15–17), and the purification of Mary after childbirth (Leviticus 12:2–5). Mary's offering of two turtledoves suggest the poverty of the holy family; a turtledove was an acceptable sacrifice for families who could not afford the requisite lamb offering (Leviticus 12:6–8).

4. Simeon's famous song of praise, the *Nunc Dimittis* (Luke 2:29–32), and Anna's proclamation to the expectant Jews can be interpreted as Temple oracles of salvation by the inspired prophets.

5. A nazarite was an individual set apart and dedicated by vows to the service of God. Nazarites abstained from drinking wine and cutting their hair.

6. We are curious about Anna's relationship with Mary. If Anna has spent the years of her widowhood praying in the Temple, she may already know Mary. According to an apocryphal gospel from the second century CE known as *The Protevangelium of James or The Nativity of Mary*, Mary's parents, Joachim and Anne, had dedicated Mary at the age of three to the service of God in the Temple, under the tutelage of the Temple priests. Mary had remained at the Temple until she was twelve, when she was then betrothed to Joseph. It is possible, then, that Anna and Mary may have come to know each other well before Mary's marriage to Joseph. When Joseph and Mary bring the baby Jesus to the Temple, the two women may enjoy a tender reunion. Perhaps Anna hears the words of Simeon to Mary, "a sword will pierce your own soul too" (Luke 2:35), and comes to Mary "at that moment" (2:38) to comfort her. Anna might also console Mary during the circumcision of Jesus, much as Jewish women today often gather round mothers during *brit milah* ceremonies.

7. Lisa Belcher Hamilton, *For Those We Love But See No Longer* (Brewster, MA: Paraclete Press), xix.

8. Barbara Cawthorne Crafton, *Almost Daily Electronic Meditations*, "A Public Service of Healing" (January 14, 2004), www.geraniumfarm.org/dailyemo.cfm?Emo=157.

Chapter 7: Judith

1. The Book of Judith is a work found in the Apocrypha, a collection of religious literature of the Jewish community written from about the third century BCE to the first century CE. The word *apocrypha* means "hidden" or "set aside." Some translations of the Bible include the Apocrypha as a separate section placed either between the Hebrew Scriptures and the New Testament or, occasionally, after the New Testament. In Catholic editions of the Bible, the books of the Apocrypha are interspersed among other books of similar type. Judith (and Tobit, another apocryphal work) comes after Nehemiah.

2. Judith's living in a tent does not appear to be a mourning practice, but rather an expression of her right relationship with God and her life of prayer. Elsewhere in the Hebrew Scriptures, tents serve as a metaphor for the prosperity of the righteous: "The house of the wicked is destroyed, but the tent of the upright flourishes" (Proverbs 14:11). Judith's tent, meanwhile, is reminiscent of the *tent of meeting*, which served as the dwelling place of God on earth before the building of the Jerusalem Temple. In the *tent of meeting*, which housed the ark of the covenant, Moses would speak with God during the people's years of wandering in the wilderness before entering the promised land (see Numbers 7:89). Similarly, Judith's tent might also be a place for personal conversations with God and, thereby, serve as an early narrative link between her and Moses, both acclaimed deliverers of Israel.

3. The scene especially resonates because Bathsheba is, herself, a biblical widow—though the circumstances of her widowhood are quite different from those of Judith. When King David watches her bathe from the roof of his house, he becomes so enticed by her beauty that he sends for her to seduce her. Bathsheba becomes pregnant as a result of this coerced sex, after which King David deliberately sends her husband, Uriah the Hittite, to the front lines of war, where he dies in battle. After Bathsheba has properly mourned Uriah's death, David marries her. God is displeased, however, and strikes their first son dead; cf. 2 Samuel, chapters 11–12.

4. Moses sings his song after the crossing of the Red Sea and the destruction of the Egyptian army (Exodus, chapter 15). Portions of both Judith's and Moses' songs of victory serve as canticles in the Daily Office liturgies of the Episcopal Church. For the Song of Moses, see *The Book of Common Prayer* (1979), 85. For the Song of Judith, see the supplemental liturgical materials presented in *Enriching Our Worship 1* (New York: Church Publishing Incorporated, 1998), 35–36.

5. Writes Eileen M. Schuller in "The Apocrypha," *The Women's Bible Commentary*, Carol A. Newsom and Sharon H. Ringe, eds. (Louisville, KY: Westminster/John Knox Press, 1992): "Judith provides an example of a female who challenges and overcomes both the male enemy and the male establishment within her own community" (243). According to Schuller, women in North American culture are especially attuned to Judith's "independent control of her estate."

6. Writes Luis Alonso-Schökel in "Judith," *Harper's Bible Commentary*, James L. May, ed. (San Francisco: HarperSanFrancisco, 1988): "She is the personification of the Jewish people. . . . She is a widow, for the Jewish nation is living at a time of grave danger and affliction, like a forlorn widow" (810). "With her unbreakable fidelity to the memory of her first husband Judith symbolizes the fidelity of the people to its only Lord. From this fidelity follows a stable peace.

Judith lives to be one hundred and five, fifteen years longer than Moses. . . . The peace she has secured lasts longer than any achieved in the times of the judges" (814).

7. This translation of the Song of Judith is from *Enriching Our Worship 1* (see note 4, above).

Chapter 8: Ruth

1. Adapted from the Declaration of Consent in the liturgy for the Celebration and Blessings of a Marriage in *The Book of Common Prayer* (1979), 424.

2. That Ruth will surprise Boaz on a threshing floor both heightens the sexual expectation and, at the same time, places their relationship within the context of God's presence and purpose. Elsewhere in Scripture, threshing floors are associated with extramarital sexual activity. The prophet Hosea warns, for example, that Israel's festive celebrations will soon end in an exile because the people are worshiping false gods: "Do not rejoice, O Israel! Do not exult as other nations do; for you have played the whore, departing from your God. You have loved a prostitute's pay on all threshing floors" (Hosea 9:1). Nevertheless, in the biblical world, a threshing floor could also be a place where divine power could become manifest; cf. 2 Samuel 6:6, Judges 6:37. The altar of the Jerusalem Temple would be located on the site of a former threshing floor purchased by King David from Ornan the Jebusite; cf. 1 Chronicles, chapters 21–22. Thus, John the Baptist's proclamation about Jesus, "His winnowing fork is in his hand, and he will clear his threshing floor and will gather his wheat into the granary; but the chaff he will burn with unquenchable fire," (Matthew 3:12, cf. Luke 3:17) foreshadows Jesus' cleansing of the Jerusalem Temple (Matthew 21:12, Mark 11:15, John 2:14–15).

3. The Hebrew words *kenaphav* and *kenaphecha* are forms of the same word, *kanaph*, which can mean either "wing" or "cloak."

4. Translation from *The Book of Common Prayer* (1979), 793.

Epilogue: Widows and Saints

1. Although women are portrayed as active leaders of the early Christian community throughout the Acts of the Apostles, Tabitha is the only woman specifically called a *disciple* of Jesus. In the entire New Testament, the feminine of the Greek word for "disciple," *mathetria*, appears only here.

2. Elijah raises the son of the widow of Zarephath (1 Kings 17:17–24); Elisha raises the son of a wealthy Shunammite woman (2 Kings 4:8–36); Jesus raises both the daughter of Jairus (Mark 5:21–43) and Lazarus (John 11:1–44).